IDIOT'S GUIDE

AS EASY AS IT G

Homemade Baby & Toddler Food

by Kimberly Aime and Natalie Weiss, RD

ALPHA

A member of Penguin Random House LLC

ALPHA BOOKS

Published by Penguin Random House LLC

Penguin Random House LLC, 375 Hudson Street, New York, New York 10014, USA · Penguin Random House LLC (Canada), 90 Eglinton Avenue East, Suite 700, Toronto, Ontario M4P 2Y3, Canada (a division of Pearson Penguin Canada Inc.) · Penguin Books Ltd., 80 Strand, London WC2R 0RL, England · Penguin Ireland, 25 St. Stephen's Green, Dublin 2, Ireland (a division of Penguin Books Ltd.) · Penguin Random House LLC (Australia), 250 Camberwell Road, Camberwell, Victoria 3124, Australia (a division of Pearson Australia Group Pty. Ltd.) · Penguin Books India Pvt. Ltd., 11 Community Centre, Panchsheel Park, New Delhi—110 017, India · Penguin Random House LLC (NZ), 67 Apollo Drive, Rosedale, North Shore, Auckland 1311, New Zealand (a division of Pearson New Zealand Ltd.) · Penguin Books (South Africa) (Pty.) Ltd., 24 Sturdee Avenue, Rosebank, Johannesburg 2196, South Africa · Penguin Books Ltd., Registered Offices: 80 Strand, London WC2R 0RL, England

001-283818-November2015

International Standard Book Number: 978-1-61564-856-6
Library of Congress Catalog Card Number: 2015904797

17 16 15   8 7 6 5 4 3 2 1

Interpretation of the printing code: The rightmost number of the first series of numbers is the year of the book's printing; the rightmost number of the second series of numbers is the number of the book's printing. For example, a printing code of 15-1 shows that the first printing occurred in 2015.

Printed and bound in China

Note: This publication contains the opinions and ideas of its author. It is intended to provide helpful and informative material on the subject matter covered. It is sold with the understanding that the author and publisher are not engaged in rendering professional services in the book. If the reader requires personal assistance or advice, a competent professional should be consulted. The author and publisher specifically disclaim any responsibility for any liability, loss, or risk, personal or otherwise, which is incurred as a consequence, directly or indirectly, of the use and application of any of the contents of this book.

Most Alpha books are available at special quantity discounts for bulk purchases for sales promotions, premiums, fund-raising, or educational use. Special books, or book excerpts, can also be created to fit specific needs. For details, write: Special Markets, Alpha Books, 375 Hudson Street, New York, NY 10014.

PUBLISHER
Mike Sanders

ASSOCIATE PUBLISHER
Billy Fields

EXECUTIVE ACQUISITIONS EDITOR
Lori Cates Hand

DEVELOPMENT EDITOR
Ann Barton

COVER AND BOOK DESIGNER
Rebecca Batchelor

PRODUCTION EDITOR
Jana M. Stefanciosa

INDEXER
Johnna VanHoose Dinse

PROOFREADER
Virginia Vasquez

PHOTOGRAPHER
Stephanie Kelley Photography

contents

PART 6

18 to 24 months. 149

introduction

Congratulations! You have decided to make your own baby and toddler food. In a time when fast and convenient are often considered better, this is a huge deal, and I applaud you.

Here is the good news: making the food is the easy part. For the first year, the hardest part about feeding your little one will be the cleanup afterward. Once you move into the age of the toddler, you'll discover your cherub is as fickle as they come. One day she'll love black beans, the next day she won't touch them. Then she'll love them again, and then she's back to hating them. It's a whirlwind to keep up!

The solution? Making meals and snacks your entire family can enjoy so you are not a short-order cook for a temperamental toddler. This book provides recipes, tips for feeding, meal plans, nutritional information, and pretty much everything else you need to know to make delicious and easy meals for your baby or toddler.

Here are some tips for getting started:

- For all of the baking recipes, you need to track down whole-wheat pastry flour—not whole-wheat flour or white whole-wheat flour. The recipes will not work well with other whole-grain flours.

- Seek out shortcuts. Your time is valuable and you should do whatever you can to make this as easy as possible. The easier it is, the more likely you are to succeed.

- If you have the time and the resources, sign up for a knife skills class in your area and invest in a good chef's knife.

- Be prepared for setbacks. It can get discouraging when your little one refuses to eat your homemade goodies. I recommend keeping a picture of your little one eating something you made. It's a nice reminder of a time when she was less picky.

helpful icons

If allergies are a concern for your family, look for the icons on each recipe indicating if a recipe is nut, egg, or dairy free. Freezer-friendly recipes are also marked.

 egg free

 nut free

 dairy free

freezer friendly

I made all of the recipes in this book while staying home with my daughter—often with her right at my side. I did not attend culinary school or work in a restaurant. I am a parent just like you. Before my daughter was born, my husband and I decided to embark on a clean-eating diet and eliminated all processed foods. In short, if it had a chemical in it, we didn't eat it. Four years later, we had our first child and we knew we wanted her to follow the same lifestyle.

I run two blogs: *Badger Girl Learns to Cook* (badgergirllearnstocook.com), a grown-up eats blog focused on clean eating and maintaining a healthy lifestyle, and *A Life Well Fed* (life-well-fed. blogspot.com), where I document our clean-eating journey as a family (no puffs allowed!) and the joys of feeding a little human. I hope you will stay in touch, and happy cooking!

–Kimberly Aime, recipe writer and developer

kimberly's *acknowledgments*

Thank you to Grace Sharon, the best little kitchen helper and recipe taster ever. Thank you to my husband, Jean-Paul, for his support and patience throughout this process. Thank you to all of my recipe testers: April Ueland, Elizabeth Krotser, Erin Racca, Lexi McArthur, Angie Richter, Nikki Dhein, Nicole Barbieri, Stefanie Freyburger, Kristen Tenney, Karin Alwin, and Jackie Monfils. Thank you to Natalie Weiss, my co-author and nutritionist. Thank you to Stephanie Kelly and the baby models for the amazing pictures, and special thanks to my editors, Lori Cates Hand and Ann Barton, for their insightful review and unending support.

natalie's *acknowledgments*

It's been an absolute delight to work on this book. A special thanks to everyone who helped make it happen: my colleague, Margaret, for getting me on board; my family, especially RJ and Halle, for all your love, support, and open-mindedness to my healthy creations; and finally to Kimberly Aime and the team at Alpha Books for making the entire process fun. Thank you all so much!

part 1

feeding and nutrition basics

As mothers, we know that transitioning your baby from breast milk or formula to baby food can be both exciting and nerve-racking. You want to do everything just right.

To make the transition as easy as possible, this section covers all the basics: when to start feeding your baby solids, how to introduce new foods, what you need to know about food allergies, how to develop a well-rounded eater, and the hot topic of baby-led weaning.

starting baby on solid foods

For most babies, it's best to start solids at around 6 months, when they've developed the motor skills to make eating easier. There's also less of a chance that baby will develop a food intolerance or allergy because her digestive system is more mature.

If you're worried about waiting so long to start solids, rest assured that breast milk or formula can meet 100 percent of a baby's nutritional needs during the first 6 months of life. Of course, every baby is different, and it may be okay for some to start solids sooner. Just be sure to discuss it with your doctor first. In the beginning, the goal of solid feedings is to introduce baby to the act of eating, not to fill her up.

First Foods

The best first foods are ones that have a low allergy risk and are appealing to little mouths. Excellent choices include sweet potato, avocado, banana, acorn squash, butternut squash, apple, pear, and infant oatmeal cereal.

Whatever food you choose, make sure it's a single element (such as plain puréed sweet potato). You can mix it with breast milk or formula to create a semi-liquid consistency. This makes the transition easier, since your baby has had only liquids up to this point.

Fruit or Vegetables First?

Some parents worry if they give fruit as a first food, their baby will refuse vegetables. I don't think this is something to feel concerned about. If your baby has been on breast milk, she's already been eating a sweet food many times each day. Offering a variety of foods is key. If you start with a fruit, try a vegetable next. Most babies will try what's put in front of them.

signs baby is ready for solids

- Can sit up in a high chair.
- Can move food to back of mouth (doesn't immediately push food out with tongue).
- Opens mouth.
- Closes mouth around spoon.
- Has good head control.
- Seems interested in food.

Feeding Your Baby for the First Time

Sit baby upright in her highchair. Place a tablespoon or two of food into a small bowl. Using an infant spoon, bring a small amount of food to baby's mouth. Continue to feed baby this way until the food is gone or until she refuses. Baby will let you know when she's done by turning her head away from the spoon or by becoming fussy in her chair.

At first, baby won't eat more than a few spoonfuls, and most of it will get on her hands rather than in her mouth. Baby will want to check out the strange new substance in her mouth. Exploration and play is common at mealtimes, and is an important part of learning how to eat.

Once eating becomes more routine, your baby's appetite will increase, and she will start to eat more. Always let your baby be your guide. Don't force her to eat when she's showing signs that she's done. Trust that your baby knows how much she needs to eat.

Meal Timing and Progression

Eating solids is a big, new adventure for your baby. To get started, try to find a time that's good for both of you. The best time for baby is when she's well-rested and hungry but not starving. For you, it's best when you don't feel rushed.

After baby's initial feeding, work up to two meals a day, and then eventually to three (breakfast, lunch, and dinner). Remember, there is no rush, and you should progress in a way that feels right for you and your baby.

It takes time to work up to three meals per day, since you will be introducing new foods one at a time with several days between.

baby-led weaning

Baby-led weaning (BLW) is a term used to describe a style of feeding where baby feeds herself right from the start. You control the what and the when, but baby decides on the how. This means you pretty much bypass the whole purée stage, and instead give baby manageable pieces of food that she can pick up and eat on her own. Parents who follow BLW believe it's a more laid-back approach to feeding, and hope it will make their child a more adventurous eater.

Is It Safe?

There is currently no research proving that BLW is more dangerous than spoon feeding a purée. Over the past few generations, it's been more common to start babies with purées. BLW is just a different approach, but it's still an acceptable way to start your baby on solid food.

By 6 months, most babies will have developed the skills to self-feed, if given the chance. According to the American Academy of Pediatrics, you can give finger foods to baby once she can sit up and bring her hands or other objects to her mouth.

For a lot of parents, the idea of giving finger foods right out the gate is daunting. However, advocates of BLW say there is no greater risk of choking than with traditional spoon-feeding methods.

BLW safety principles

According to Gill Rapley, author of *Baby-Led Weaning*:

- Sit baby upright to eat.
- Don't give baby whole nuts.
- Cut small fruits such as cherries in half, and take out any pits.
- Baby is the only one to put food in her mouth.
- Inform caregivers on how BLW works.
- Never leave baby alone with food.

advantages of BLW

- No need to prepare separate purées for baby.

- You get two hands to eat your own meal.

- Encourages independence and exploration.

disadvantages of BLW

- Very messy.

- Wasted food.

- Not much food makes it into baby's tummy at first.

What Foods Does Baby Eat?

With BLW, you encourage baby to take part in family meals and share table foods. Things like fruits, vegetables, meat, cheese, eggs, bread or toast, fish, rice, and pasta are common foods given to baby.

The food must be prepared in a way that's easy for baby to eat. For example, cook hard vegetables so they're soft enough for baby to chew. It's best to offer foods that are baby-fist-sized and have a natural handle (such as a broccoli floret). Cutting food into strips works well, too.

Just as in traditional baby feeding, variety is a key component to help baby adapt to new flavors and textures.

A baby just starting on the BLW method may spend a lot of time exploring the food at first, but with time she will learn to chew and swallow it.

Is Baby-Led Weaning Right for You?

The best part of being a parent is that you get to decide how to bring up your baby. Don't feel like you need to subscribe to any particular method. Only you can decide what's best for your baby and your lifestyle.

You can go by baby's cues, too. Some babies will try to grab the spoon and feed themselves. This is a sign that they might enjoy more foods to pick up and eat.

As a mother and registered dietitian, a combination of purées and finger foods makes the most sense to me. The purées help ensure good nutrition and the finger foods help build chewing ability and independence. To learn more about BLW, visit Gill Rapley's website, rapleyweaning.com.

introducing new foods

After baby's first feeding, you may be wondering what to do next. The general rule of thumb is to introduce one new food at a time and wait three days between each new food. The waiting period makes it easier to spot any potential food allergies or intolerances.

There used to be specific guidelines on the order of introducing new foods, but a lot has changed in the past few years. With a few exceptions, any food is fair game for your baby, as long as you prepare it in a way she can handle.

Foods to Avoid in the First Year

There are a few foods you shouldn't give your baby before she turns 1.

Honey: The botulism bacteria often contaminates honey. A baby's digestive system is too immature to properly fight off this bacteria. Honey does not cause sickness in children over age 1.

Cow's milk: Cow's milk can be irritating to a baby's young digestive system. It also has a higher protein load than breast milk or formula, which can stress the kidneys. Yogurt and cheese are okay to give before age 1.

Choking hazards: Examples include chunks of raw vegetables, hot dogs, whole nuts and seeds, whole grapes, popcorn, chunks of nut butter, and chunks of meat or cheese.

introducing new textures

It's important to keep baby progressing with new textures. This helps her prepare for more independent eating. Every baby progresses in her own way, but here's what you should aim for.

5 to 6 months
Single-food purées + mashed foods

7 to 8 months
Complex purées + finger foods

Building Healthy Habits

Try not to stress too much about serving sizes and calories. Baby is still getting at least half of her nutritional needs met by breast milk or formula. To develop a well-rounded eater, it's better to focus on variety, taste, and texture.

One of the best things you can do to ensure the healthfulness of the food you give to baby is to make it yourself! This way, you know exactly what's going into baby's mouth, and baby will love the taste of fresh food.

Remember that you're the best role model for baby. If she sees you turning your nose up at kale, why would she want to try it? Although it can be difficult to coordinate with baby's schedule, try to sit down and eat with her as much as possible. This gives baby valuable information about how to eat and act at the table.

What About Drinks?

Baby's primary beverage is formula or breast milk until age 1. If she drinks too many other liquids throughout the day, she won't get her essential nutrition. When baby starts eating solid foods, you can give her a small amount of water in a sippy cup at mealtimes. It's not for hydration, but rather for learning how to drink from a cup.

It's not necessary to give baby any juice. She'll get more valuable nutrition from eating actual fruit. Think of juice more as a treat than an everyday necessity, and if you do give it, select 100 percent juice varieties with no added sugar.

feeding and nutrition basics

9 to 11 months
Chunkier foods + finger foods

12 to 17 months
Pieces of table food

18 to 24 months
Toddler meals

choosing organic foods

Shoppers entering a supermarket today are faced with a bewildering number of food options, and figuring out what's best for your family can feel overwhelming. As a parent with a little one to feed, you may be wondering about organics now more than ever.

What Does Organic Mean?

The USDA defines *organic* as crops grown without using most synthetically derived pesticides, petroleum-based fertilizers, or sewage sludge–based fertilizers. (Organic farms can, however, use naturally derived pesticides from a list approved by the Natural Organic Standards Board, as well as natural fertilizers.)

Animals raised on an organic farm eat organic feed and must be able to go outside. They are not given antibiotics or growth hormones. Organic regulations do not allow the use of genetic engineering (GMOs) or ionizing radiation.

Organic farms must go through a certification process to ensure they meet regulations. They're either certified by the USDA or a USDA-accredited agency. Only certified organic farms can use the USDA organic seal.

The Problem with Pesticides

One of the many reasons more and more parents are deciding to go organic is to avoid exposure to synthetically derived pesticides.

According to the Natural Resources Defense Council, the use of pesticides has increased by 50 percent over the past 30 years. This has occurred as a result of the shift from small family farms to large industrial farms.

The effects of pesticide exposure are not completely understood, but there is evidence to suggest that it can be linked to cancer, birth defects, reproductive issues, neurological problems, immune system disruption, and hormonal imbalances.

The Environmental Protection Agency states that pesticides pose a greater risk to infants and children. A child's organ system is still growing, they eat and

how to spot organic products

- Look for the green-and-white USDA organic seal.

- Check out produce stickers. If the code starts with the number 9, it's certified organic.

drink more per body weight than adults, and through play they have more contact with soil and plants that may contain pesticides.

Feeding your child organic foods can help get rid of pesticides in their body in a short amount of time. In one study published by the National Institute of Environmental Health Sciences, researchers replaced children's typical food with organic food for five consecutive days. After testing their urine for 15 days, they found that an organic diet caused a dramatic and immediate reduction in common pesticides.

When to Buy Organic

It's difficult to make your child's diet 100 percent organic. Instead, focus on the areas that will make the biggest difference. Produce is one place to start. The Environmental Working Group has identified 13 fruits and vegetables that have particularly high levels of residual pesticides. Buying these organic will help to reduce your child's exposure to synthetic pesticides. Another option is to swap out the foods your child eats most frequently with organic versions.

When in doubt, remember that fresh is best. A non-organic fresh fruit or vegetable is better for your child than a packaged organic snack food like cheese crackers or fruit snacks.

foods to buy organic

- Apples
- Strawberries
- Grapes
- Celery
- Peaches
- Spinach
- Potatoes
- Sweet bell peppers and hot peppers
- Nectarines
- Cucumbers
- Cherry tomatoes
- Snap peas
- Kale and collard greens

From the Environmental Working Group's 2014 Dirty Dozen List

food allergies

Now that your baby is starting to eat solid food, allergies may be one of your top concerns. Over the past decade, food allergies have been on the rise, and it's estimated that around 8 percent of children have a food allergy.

Preventing Food Allergies

The recommendations regarding food allergies have changed in recent years. In the past, doctors told parents to wait to introduce the top allergy-producing foods in order to lower the risk of food allergies. However, in 2008, the American Academy of Pediatrics did a review of research and concluded there was no convincing evidence for waiting to introduce these foods.

Some experts think that waiting to introduce foods may have the opposite effect, and increase the chance of food allergy. More recent research even suggests that starting allergenic foods early on may help to prevent food allergies in babies and children.

Exclusive breastfeeding for at least 6 months may offer some protection against allergies, but avoiding allergenic foods while breastfeeding will not help prevent food allergies. If breast milk cannot be the sole food for baby during the first four months, a formula with broken-down proteins (called hydrolyzed) may help prevent allergies.

Introducing Allergenic Foods

It's recommended that all babies start on solid foods at around 6 months. Waiting any longer will not reduce the risk of developing a food allergy. When introducing food for the first time, you don't want to start with any of the top allergenic foods. Once baby has tried and tolerated a few of the typical first foods, you can start to introduce an allergenic food.

When introducing one of the allergenic foods, just give baby a small taste or bite. Wait several hours or even until the next day to monitor for any reactions. If baby seems fine, you can gradually increase the amount you give over time. It's best to introduce allergenic foods at home, instead of at a daycare or restaurant.

the top 8 allergenic foods

1. Cow's milk
2. Eggs
3. Peanuts
4. Tree nuts
5. Fish
6. Shellfish
7. Soy
8. Wheat

What Does an Allergy Look Like?

If your child reacts to a particular food, you will know. Signs usually appear immediately or within hours. Look for hives, welts, skin rashes, swelling of the face or tongue, vomiting, diarrhea, coughing, wheezing, difficulty breathing, and loss of consciousness.

If your child has difficulty breathing or loses consciousness, immediately call for emergency assistance. In all other cases of a suspected reaction, consult your child's doctor for instruction on what to do next.

Dealing with a food allergy can be difficult, but the good news is that many kids outgrow them before they reach adolescence. There are also many excellent resources and food products available for food allergies.

Special Situations

If food allergies or other allergies run in your family, consult your pediatrician about how to introduce the top allergy-producing foods. He or she may have special instructions or give you a referral to see an allergist.

did you know?
A child with a sibling who has a peanut allergy is seven times more likely to have one herself.

Food Sensitivities

Some babies have mild reactions to foods that can have you second guessing whether it's a food allergy. Food sensitivities (also called intolerances) tend to cause dull reactions that develop slowly over time. This often makes it hard to figure out the offending food. Signs of a food intolerance may show up days after eating a problematic food. With a food sensitivity, you may see things like nausea, stomach pain, gas, cramps, vomiting, acid reflux, and loose stools.

One of the best ways to spot a food intolerance is to keep a food journal of everything baby eats, noting baby's behavior and any physical symptoms. Over time you may see a pattern developing. From there, avoid the suspected food for a week, checking for improvements. After a week, introduce the food again and see what happens. The top allergenic foods are also the foods most likely to cause an intolerance.

It's common for acidic fruits like berries, tomatoes, and citrus to irritate baby's skin and cause redness around the mouth. In this type of reaction, the redness or rash doesn't spread beyond the mouth. This is not considered to be an allergy or intolerance unless other symptoms are present.

encouraging picky eaters

Why is it that some kids eat everything under the sun and others seem to live off bread, cereal, and cheese? A lot of factors are at play, but one thing is for certain: at some point, most children go through a picky phase. This is a normal (if frustrating) part of childhood. The goal is to keep it mild and short-lived.

Encourage Variety Early On

Most babies are adventurous eaters if given the opportunity. Around age 2, they start to become more cautious about the food they eat. This stage can last until age 6. During this time, rejection of vegetables is likely to reach an all-time high. One of the best things you can do is offer baby many new foods, textures, and flavors before age 2. This will help her be more accepting of food, even as she enters the common picky stage.

Don't Give Up Too Soon

When it comes to a rejected food, many parents give up way too soon. Your little one may need to see, touch, or taste a food 20 or more times before she learns to like it.

Also keep in mind that baby's preferences and appetite can vary from day to day. Maybe she liked peas yesterday but refuses to eat them today. Or maybe she tried everything on her plate at dinner, but only wants to eat toast for breakfast. These things are all normal.

As long as you continue to offer healthy meals, with a variety of foods, you are doing the right thing. Rest assured that baby has a good internal barometer about what and when she needs to eat.

How to Raise an Adventurous Eater

do:

- **Introduce as many flavors and textures as possible before age 2.** This can help to reduce picky eating later on.

- **Be a good role model.** Eat the foods you want your baby to eat. She will learn from you.

- **Let your child get hungry.** So many times, pickiness just means they filled up on something else, often snacks. Scheduled mealtimes can help end too much snacking.

- **Flavor baby's food with herbs and spices.** Toddlers love dunking foods in sauces and dips, too.

- **Add vegetables to meals you know baby already loves.** If soup is a winner, try adding in some more vegetables. Smoothies are another great place to add in nutrition.

- **Try preparing the same food different ways.** A toddler who hates mashed sweet potato might love baked sweet potato fries!

- **Keep offering a food baby has refused in the past.** Maybe after the fifteenth time, it will start to look good and she will try it.

- **Offer a variety of healthy foods at meals.** Aim for a protein, a vegetable, and a starch.

don't:

- **Use food as a punishment or a reward.** This creates unhealthy beliefs about food.

- **Make a big deal of baby's food preferences.** This will lead to a power struggle between you and baby, and make her less likely to ever try a new food.

- **Offer to make something "special" if your child refuses a meal.** This will give her the idea that she can always have a different meal if she doesn't like what you've prepared.

- **Offer more than two choices for a meal.** Say, "Would you like eggs or oatmeal for breakfast?" not, "What would you like for breakfast?"

- **Keep a lot of junk food in the house.** If it's there, your child will ask or possibly beg for it.

- **Force your child to eat anything.** But don't let it stop you from offering the food again! One day, she may want to try it.

tools for making your own baby food

There are two steps to making your own puréed baby food: softening the food, usually by steaming or roasting, and processing the food to a purée consistency. These steps can be accomplished using several different methods. You can decide which techniques work best in your kitchen. Here are some tools you may need.

Slow cooker: Prepping your food in a slow cooker is the most hands-off method you can use. You don't have to worry about overcooking; just prep and walk away. When you are ready for the next step, retrieve the food and proceed. This method is particularly good for foods that take a little longer to soften, like sweet potatoes, squash, and carrots.

Microwave steamer: Another quick way to prep fruits and veggies for purées is with a fresh produce microwave steamer. You can steam your produce in minutes, and you only have a single bowl to wash.

Steamer insert: If you prefer stovetop cooking, you can steam food using a saucepan with a steamer insert.

Sheet pan: A sheet pan can be used to roast fruits or vegetables to soften them. Line with parchment paper or foil for easy cleanup.

Immersion blender: Immersion blenders are perfect for small batches of purées. They process food quickly and are easier to clean than full-size blenders.

Blender: For bigger batches of purées, a full-size blender is best.

Food processor: While I don't recommend them for purées, food processors are great for prepping toddler foods and family meals.

Freezer containers: Most purées freeze well, so it's a good idea to have a variety of freezer containers available. I recommend using silicone ice cube trays as well as containers that come with a lid. The lidded containers are great for going from freezer directly to diaper bag for meals on the go.

Dissolvable labels: You can find dissolvable food labels in the canning department. These are useful for labeling purées or any leftovers because the label will dissolve when you wash the container.

other helpful tools

Vegetable peeler: When your little one is ready for finger food, it helps to have a good vegetable peeler to remove the skins from apples, cucumbers, and other produce.

Pizza cutter: A pizza cutter is a great tool for cutting just about anything into bite-size pieces.

Spiralizer: This fun tool cuts vegetables into noodle-like shapes that you can toss with regular pasta and sauce or serve on their own.

make it work for you!

This book is designed to show you how easy and hands-off making your own baby food can be. Many parents start out trying to be perfect and become so overwhelmed that they quit.

In order to be successful at making your own baby food, use every shortcut you can find. If that means using your microwave or slow cooker so you're not standing over a stove, do it!

part 2

5 to 6 months

Fun times are ahead! Starting solids is one of the most exciting milestones in baby's first year. When your baby starts eating food, you have a great new way to interact together. At first, your baby won't eat very much, so it's easy to start making your own baby food. In this section, you'll learn what baby should be eating, as well as everything you need to know about making your own purées.

what baby is eating now: *simple purées*

Simple purée is the term used to describe the first foods fed to baby. A simple purée contains only one food, and has a silky-smooth texture. A simple purée can be a nice transition for baby, since he's only had liquids up to this point. Among store-bought baby foods, simple purées are known as "stage 1" foods.

How to Feed Your Baby

- Place a small amount of your prepared purée into a small bowl or jar. Two ounces (55g) or ¼ cup is a good starting place.

- Dip an infant spoon into the purée and bring it a few inches from baby's lips.

- When he opens his mouth, begin to feed him. Make sure to give him lots of time to adapt to this new experience.

- Stop when he's finished.

- Wait 3 to 5 days before introducing a new food. Some babies will try to grab the spoon to self-feed. If this is the case, help him guide the spoon into his mouth.

When to Feed Your Baby

The progression to solid foods is slow. At 5 to 6 months, breast milk or formula will continue to make up the majority of baby's diet. Start with one meal a day, and increase when you think baby is ready. By the end of 6 months, most babies will be at two meals per day. The frequency and amount depends on your baby and his daily routine.

nutritional note

To increase the nutritional value of your purées, use the water in which you cooked the food to blend it up. You can also use fresh breast milk or formula to thin out purées as needed.

nutritional needs: 5 to 6 *months*

Baby has been growing by leaps and bounds. He has been gaining about an ounce (25g) per day, and has likely doubled his birth weight. At 6 months, weight gain will start to slow to about 1 pound (450g) per month.

Though growth is slowing, baby still needs lots of nutrition. The requirements for several key nutrients increase, including iron, phosphorus, vitamin C, vitamin A, and calcium. He also needs more calories and protein than before. These needs will be met by the introduction of solid foods into his diet.

Breast milk or formula is still the bulk of baby's diet, with 4 to 6 feeding sessions per day (28 to 32 ounces [830 to 950ml]). Once you start introducing foods, baby will take less breast milk or formula. The transition isn't quick; it happens slowly over time.

Nutrition Spotlight: Vitamin A

Vitamin A is an important nutrient for infants and children. It ensures proper development of eyes and bones, protects the body from infections, and helps the heart, lungs, and kidneys work their best. Infants and children have higher vitamin A requirements per body weight than adults. That's why it's important to make sure your child is getting enough.

Vitamin A is found in many plant and animal foods. Orange, yellow, and green fruits and vegetables are rich in vitamin A. Animal products, such as dairy, meat, and some fish also contain vitamin A. Your baby is still getting a lot of vitamin A in breast milk or formula, but after 6 months, he needs more vitamin A from food. Luckily, many of baby's early favorite foods are rich in this essential nutrient.

RECIPE TO TRY: Carrots and Cumin Purée

foods rich in vitamin A

Sweet potato

Spinach

Kale

Carrots

Pumpkin

Cantaloupe

Mangoes

Apricots

Broccoli

Papaya

Bell peppers

Dairy products

Salmon

meal plans:
5 to 6 months

Here are daily and weekly plans for feeding your baby at this stage. Keep in mind that every baby is different. This is only meant to be a guide, not a strict schedule.

Sample Feeding Schedule

TIME	SLEEP AND FOOD
6:00–6:30 AM	Baby wakes up and is nursed or bottle-fed.
8:00–8:30 AM	Baby naps for 1 to 1½ hours.
9:00–9:30 AM	Baby wakes up and is nursed or bottle-fed.
10:30 AM	Mid-morning meal: oatmeal mixed with breast milk or formula + fruit purée **or** fruit purée + vegetable purée
11:30 AM–1:00 PM	Baby naps for 1½ to 2 hours.
1:00–1:30 PM	Baby wakes and is nursed or bottle-fed.
3:00–3:30 PM	Baby naps 45 minutes to 1 hour.
4:00–4:30 PM	Baby wakes up and is nursed or bottle-fed.
5:30–6:00 PM	Dinner: vegetable purée + fruit purée
7:00–7:30 PM	Nurse or bottle-feed before bed.

notes

- When oatmeal is mentioned in the meal plan, feel free to use baby whole-grain oats or regular oats. Baby oatmeal doesn't require cooking and is usually fortified with iron. Regular oatmeal should be cooked and puréed with formula or fresh breast milk to a smooth consistency.

- When possible, try to batch cook your purées. It will save you time. Sunday is a great day to get ahead on cooking for the week.

- Keep quick fixes on hand if baby refuses to eat a specific purée. Bananas and avocados can be eaten right out of the skin, and sweet potatoes can be microwaved for a quick meal.

- Don't throw out leftover frozen purées that baby doesn't like. Repurpose them for later use. Once baby starts eating more, they can be added to other meals.

Sample Weekly Meal Plan

DAY	MEALS
Monday	**Mid-morning meal:** 2–4 TB. oatmeal mixed with breast milk or formula + 2 TB. peach purée **Dinner:** 2–4 TB. sweet potato purée + 2 TB. apple purée
Tuesday	**Mid-morning meal:** 2–4 TB. oatmeal mixed with breast milk or formula + 2 TB. pear purée **Dinner:** 2–4 TB. zucchini purée + 2 TB. apple purée
Wednesday	**Mid-morning meal:** 2–4 TB. oatmeal mixed with breast milk or formula + 2 TB. mashed banana **Dinner:** 2–4 TB. butternut squash + 2 TB. pear purée
Thursday	**Mid-morning meal:** 2–4 TB. oatmeal mixed with breast milk or formula + 2 TB. pear purée **Dinner:** 2–4 TB. sweet potato purée + 2 TB. peach purée
Friday	**Mid-morning meal:** 2–4 TB. oatmeal mixed with breast milk or formula + 2 TB. mashed banana **Dinner:** 2–4 TB. zucchini purée + 2 TB. apple purée
Saturday	**Mid-morning meal:** 2–4 TB. oatmeal mixed with breast milk or formula + 2 TB. peach purée **Dinner:** 2–4 TB. butternut squash purée + 2 TB. mashed avocado
Sunday	**Mid-morning meal:** 2–4 TB. oatmeal mixed with breast milk or formula + 2 TB. pear purée **Dinner:** 2–4 TB. sweet potato purée + 2 TB. mashed avocado

making purées

When making a purée, your goal is to soften the food and then blend it to a consistency that is smooth enough for your toothless little one to enjoy. Some soft fruits (mangoes, strawberries, blueberries, blackberries, watermelon) can go directly in the blender, no pre-cooking required. Harder fruits and vegetables need to be softened by steaming or roasting.

Softening Methods

There are several ways to soften food for purées. The method you choose will depend on the time and tools you have available, as well as the size of the batch you plan to make and the fruits and veggies you're using. My two preferred methods are microwave steaming and cooking in the slow cooker.

Microwave Steaming

AVERAGE TIME	3 to 10 minutes	HANDS-ON TIME (EXCLUDING CHOPPING)	1 to 2 minutes

Wash produce and peel if needed. Cut into 2 to 3-inch (5–7.5cm) chunks.

Add 1 to 1½ cups water to the reservoir in the fresh produce microwave steamer. Place the produce in the basket. Microwave on high for 3 to 8 minutes, or until fork-tender. Carrots generally take 8 to 10 minutes. More delicate produce, like green beans or broccoli, will be ready in 3 to 4 minutes.

Place steamed ingredients in a blender with some or all of the steaming water. Purée until you reach the desired consistency. For younger babies and for using in pouches, you want a smooth purée. For older kids, you can have a thicker, chunkier purée.

Other Methods

Slow-cooker steaming: Place 3 to 10 cups fruit or vegetable chunks in a slow cooker with ¼ to ½ cup water or liquid. Cook on low for 2 to 4 hours or until tender. This method is particularly good for firmer vegetables like squash, sweet potatoes, and carrots.

AVERAGE TIME	2 to 4 hours	HANDS-ON TIME (EXCLUDING CHOPPING)	1 to 2 minutes

Stovetop steaming: Using a steam basket insert, steam cut-up veggies or fruit over boiling water until tender.

AVERAGE TIME	15 to 30 minutes	HANDS-ON TIME (EXCLUDING CHOPPING)	15 minutes

Roasting: Toss fruit or vegetable chunks with 1 TB. oil or butter and spread on a baking sheet. Roast at 400°F (200°C) until fork-tender. This method is good for root vegetables and can also bring out the sweetness and flavor of fruits.

AVERAGE TIME	2 to 4 hours	HANDS-ON TIME (EXCLUDING CHOPPING)	1 to 2 minutes

beyond fruits and vegetables

Experiment with adding meat and grains to your purées for more flavor and protein. Here are some tips for preparation.

Chicken: Place chicken breasts in a medium saucepan. Cover with 1 inch (3cm) water. Add carrots and celery for more flavor, if desired. Bring to a simmer over medium-high heat, then cover and reduce to low for 20 minutes. Internal temperature should be 165°F (74°C). Purée in the blender with some of the poaching liquid or a little broth.

Beef: Place beef roast in a slow cooker. You can also add carrots and celery for more flavor and a more complex purée. Cover with half broth and half water. Cook on low for 7 to 8 hours until beef is fork-tender. Purée in the blender with some of the liquid from the slow cooker.

Grains: Cook grains according to package directions. You may want to add an additional ¼ to ½ cup vegetable broth to aid in puréeing. Suggested grains include quinoa, brown rice, and couscous.

freezing purées

To make your life easier, get into the habit of freezing some of your purées whenever you make a batch. This will give you a rainy-day stash of food.

Containers for Freezing

Silicone ice cube trays: The easiest way to freeze purées is to use a simple silicone ice cube tray. After they are frozen, transfer to a freezer bag.

Pouches: Pouches are great space savers for big stocks of purées. Freeze them flat and then stick them in a rectangular plastic container standing vertically. Or just throw them in a large zipper-lock freezer bag. Pouches are great for feeding your little one on the go.

Freezer containers: Several companies market little freezer-safe containers for purées. These are great for going from the freezer right to your diaper bag, but they can be expensive and are not as space saving as the other two options.

How to Freeze Purées

Make the purée.

If the purée is hot, cool at room temperature for 5 to 10 minutes and then transfer to the fridge to cool completely. Once cooled, transfer to pouches, silicone ice cube trays, or lidded freezer containers.

Freeze for at least 24 hours. If using silicone ice cube trays, transfer frozen purée cubes to a labeled freezer-safe zipper-lock bag. Store frozen purées for up to 3 months.

Tips for Freezing Purées

When it comes to freezing purées, there are a few important things to remember:

Label, label, label. Always label what you put in the freezer. Include the type of purée and the date it was frozen. If you are using pouches, label the pouches. If you are using ice cube trays, write the label for the zipper-lock bag when you are putting the purée in the ice cube tray. Then it's just a matter of transferring the frozen purée to the designated bag.

Keep a list of what's in your freezer. It's easy to build up a stock of purées and then totally forget about them. Keep a running list so you know what you have and what you've used.

thawing frozen purées

There are a few methods for thawing frozen purées. You can thaw overnight in the fridge. If you're leaving for the day and will need the purée at lunch (or in a few hours), throw the frozen container in your diaper bag and it should be thawed by the time you need it. If you need a purée thawed quickly, put the purée container in a bowl of warm water for about 10 minutes. Thawing in the microwave is not recommended due to the risk of hot spots in the purée.

single-food purées

A number of different fruits and vegetables can be softened by steaming or roasting (if needed) and then puréed in the blender and served on their own. Here are some sure bets to try:

Apples: Often baby's first solid food. Sweeter, softer varieties are easiest to purée.

Apricots: You can make this purée from fresh, dried, or canned apricots. If using canned apricots, make sure the apricots are packed in fruit juice or water, not corn syrup.

Blueberries: Because of seeds and skin, this purée isn't absolutely smooth; therefore, it's best to wait until baby is used to eating from a spoon to introduce it.

Broccoli: Introduce broccoli early to get baby used to this important staple of a healthy diet.

Butternut squash: Many babies enjoy this vitamin-A-loaded veggie.

Carrots: Because of their sweetness, this is a favorite baby vegetable.

Peaches: This fruit makes a runny purée that is suitable for introducing early. It's best to use fresh or frozen peaches rather than canned.

Pears: Choose ripe Bartlett or D'Anjou pears for a less-grainy purée.

Peas: Use frozen baby peas. Due to texture, hold off on introducing until baby's tastes are established.

Plums: Choose ripe plums that give a little when pressed gently.

Spinach: This is a great source of vitamins A, C, and K, as well as iron. Add breast milk or formula to sweeten this purée.

Sweet potatoes: Sweet potatoes purée easily and provide generous amounts of vitamin A.

apples

butternut squash

peas

carrots

pears

5 to 6 months

mashed foods

Mashes are great when you're out of purées and you need to whip up something quickly. The slightly lumpy texture is also a good stepping stone for learning how to chew. Here are some foods that can be quickly mashed with a fork to the right consistency; no blender required.

avocado

No-Cook Mashes

Avocado

Banana

Canned beans

Mango (extra ripe and peeled)

Pears (extra ripe and peeled)

bananas

Cooked Mashes

Apples: Peel and slice into quarters. Place in a fresh produce microwave steamer. Microwave on high for 3 to 5 minutes until fork-tender.

Parsnips and carrots: Peel and slice into 2-inch (5cm) pieces. Place in a fresh produce microwave steamer. Microwave on high for 10 to 12 minutes until fork-tender.

Peas: Place a handful of frozen peas in a glass bowl, cover with a glass or ceramic plate, and microwave on high for 1 to 2 minutes.

Potatoes: Pierce holes in the skin with a fork and microwave on high for 5 to 6 minutes. If mashed potato seems dry, mix in breast milk or formula.

Squash (butternut, acorn, and spaghetti): Cut in half and scoop out seeds. Place in a cake pan with a few tablespoons of water, cut side down. Bake at 400°F (200°C) for 35 to 75 minutes, depending on the size of the squash. Test doneness by piercing with a fork. When it's tender to the touch, remove.

Sweet potatoes: Pierce holes in the skin with a fork and microwave on high for 5 to 6 minutes.

applesauce *with cinnamon*

PREP	10 to 20 minutes
COOK	4 hours
YIELD	6 cups
SPECIAL TOOLS	slow cooker

This is a great early purée for your little one. Peeling the apples will yield a smooth, light-colored purée, but if you have a high-powered blender like a Vitamix, you can leave the skins on and still achieve a smooth texture.

10 medium apples, peeled and sliced

½ cup water

3 cinnamon sticks

1. Place apples, water, and cinnamon sticks in a medium slow cooker. Cook on low for 4 hours or until apples are fork-tender. Remove cinnamon sticks.

2. Transfer half of the cooked apple mixture to a blender. Purée until you reach the desired consistency. Pour into storage or freezer containers and repeat with the remainder of the apple mixture.

3. Refrigerate in an airtight container for up to 1 week or store in the freezer for up to 3 months.

carrots *and cumin*

PREP	5 minutes
COOK	8 to 10 minutes
YIELD	2 cups

Carrots are naturally sweet and are a great starter purée for your little one. The cumin adds a touch of savory flavor and is a nice way to start introducing spices. By using baby carrots, you eliminate all prep work.

3 cups baby carrots (or 3 medium carrots, peeled and chopped)

1 cup water

¼ tsp. ground cumin

1. Place the carrots in the basket of a fresh produce microwave steamer. Pour 1 cup water in the reservoir. Microwave on high for 8 to 10 minutes or until the carrots are fork-tender. Reserve steaming water.

2. Put carrots, steaming water, and cumin in a blender and blend until smooth.

3. Store in an airtight container in the fridge for up to 1 week or in the freezer for up to 3 months.

nutritional note

Applesauce is a great food to try on sore or upset tummies, especially if it's made without the skin of the apples. It's easy to tolerate and is rich in a type of fiber called pectin, which may help slow diarrhea in babies.

part 3

7 to 8 months

At 7 to 8 months, eating has become part of your little one's daily routine. Baby's appetite is increasing, and she's working up to three meals per day. Now that you've tried a bunch of simple purées, you can begin to create some combination purées. If baby seems interested in feeding herself, it's also a great time to try some age-appropriate finger foods. In this section, you'll find suggestions for finger foods to try and some tasty purée combinations that baby will love.

what baby is eating now: *complex purées and finger foods*

Babies develop so quickly. Just when you get the hang of things, it's time to change again. Eating is no exception. Your little one is ready now to begin exploring complex purées and finger foods.

New Things to Try

Purée combinations: We call these "complex purées." It's a purée made up of more than one food. Baby will love new flavors to try, and the variety will add more nutrition to her meals.

Age-appropriate finger foods: These include soft, peeled fruits and soft, cooked veggies. Finger foods teach baby how to chew and swallow, and encourage fine motor skills.

A sippy cup: This is more for educational purposes than hydration. It takes time to master the skill of cup drinking. Fill it with a few ounces of breast milk, formula, or water and give to baby with her meals. Water is great to start with because baby won't drink much at first.

Puréed meats: Meat is rich in iron and zinc, two nutrients baby needs more of after 6 months.

Don't force baby into anything she's not ready for. If she doesn't seem interested in feeding herself, you can hold off on the finger foods. Give it a try and see how baby reacts; you might be surprised.

Planning Balanced Meals

Your kiddo is becoming more hungry, so be prepared to offer more food and a greater variety. At this age, most babies are taking three meals per day. To ensure balanced nutrition, use these simple guidelines to plan baby's meals.

Breakfast: Cereal + fruit
Example: Whole-grain baby oatmeal + applesauce

Lunch: Protein + starch + vegetable
Example: Purée of chicken and sweet potato + soft-cooked broccoli chunks

Dinner: Protein + vegetable + fruit or starch
Example: Purée of white beans, spinach, and carrot + peeled, very ripe pear chunks (or purée)

nutritional needs: 7 to 8 *months*

At 7 months, average weight gain is about 3 to 5 ounces (80–140g) per week, or about 1 pound (450g) per month. Baby's primary nutrition source remains breast milk or formula. Most babies this age are still taking 24 to 32 ounces (710–950ml) per day, or nursing up to five times.

Baby's appetite for solid foods may be increasing now that meals are routine, and she's starting to get more active. Every bite counts, so make sure you're providing foods with lots of nutrition. Here are some approximate serving sizes for this age.

Fruits: ¼ cup per day

Whole grains: ¼ cup per day

Vegetables: ¼ cup per day

Meat and protein-rich foods: 1 to 2 tablespoons per day

Nutrition Spotlight: Iron

Iron is a mineral the body uses to make special proteins that carry oxygen from the lungs to all other body parts. It's essential for growth and development. Low iron levels in infants and toddlers can lead to delayed development, social withdrawal, and inability to pay attention.

Healthy, full-term babies are born with enough iron stores to last them at least six months. Around 7 months, your baby needs more iron because her stores begin to run out. She can get all the iron she needs from breast milk or formula and iron-rich foods.

Iron is found in both plant and animal foods. It's more easily absorbed when it comes from animal sources. Vitamin C also helps baby absorb more iron from food, so try to pair vitamin C–rich foods with iron-rich foods. Vitamin C–rich foods include citrus, strawberries, bell peppers, tomatoes, and broccoli.

RECIPES TO TRY:
Chicken, Kale, and Sweet Potato Purée (pictured)
Indian-Spiced Black Bean and Spinach Purée

foods rich in iron

Beef

Pork

Chicken

Turkey

Beans

Lentils

Dark green leafy vegetables, like spinach

Puréed unsweetened dried fruits, like raisins and apricots

Egg yolks

Peas

meal plans:
7 to 8 months

Here are daily and weekly meal plans for feeding your baby at this stage. Keep in mind that every baby is different. This is only meant to be a guide, not a strict schedule.

Sample Feeding Schedule

TIME	SLEEP AND FOOD
6:30–7:00 AM	Baby wakes and is nursed or bottle-fed.
7:30–8:00 AM	Breakfast: oatmeal + fruit **or** fruit + vegetable
9:00 AM	Baby naps for 1 hour.
10:00 AM	Baby wakes and is nursed or bottle-fed.
11:30 AM	Lunch: protein + veggie + starch or fruit
1:00 PM	Baby naps 1 to 2 hours.
2:00–3:00 PM	Baby wakes and is nursed or bottle-fed.
4:30 PM	Baby may have a third nap. The third nap is variable at this stage.
5:00–5:30 PM	Dinner: protein + veggie + starch or fruit
7:00–7:30 PM	Nurse or bottle-feed before bedtime.

Meal Key

Protein = meat, eggs, beans, lentils, yogurt, and cheese

Starch = whole grains, potatoes, peas, winter squash (butternut, acorn), and corn

Veggie = any vegetable other than peas, potatoes, winter squash, or corn

- Plan baby's purées around what you're having for dinner. If you're having chicken, roasted broccoli, and mashed potatoes, make a purée for baby from the chicken and broccoli, and give her a small side of the mashed potatoes.

- Serve water in a sippy cup with meals.

- If you have leftover single purées in your freezer, you can still use those to whip up a meal for baby.

Sample Weekly Meal Plan

DAY	MEALS
Monday	**Breakfast:** 2–4 TB. oatmeal + 2 TB. Cranberry Apple Pear Purée **Lunch:** 1–2 TB. Homemade Yogurt, 1–2 TB. grated or puréed cucumber, 1–2 TB. mashed avocado **Dinner:** 2–4 TB. Chicken, Kale, and Sweet Potato Purée
Tuesday	**Breakfast:** 2–4 TB. oatmeal + 2 TB. Cranberry Apple Pear Purée **Lunch:** 2–4 TB. Chicken, Kale, and Sweet Potato Purée **Dinner:** 2–4 TB. Quinoa, Chickpea, Apple, and Veggies Purée
Wednesday	**Breakfast:** 2–4 TB. oatmeal + 2 TB. Cranberry Apple Pear Purée **Lunch:** 2–4 TB. Chicken, Kale, and Sweet Potato Purée **Dinner:** 2–4 TB. Quinoa, Chickpea, Apple, and Veggies Purée
Thursday	**Breakfast:** 2–4 TB. oatmeal + 2 TB. Cranberry Apple Pear Purée **Lunch:** 2–4 TB. Chicken, Kale, and Sweet Potato Purée **Dinner:** 2–4 TB. Quinoa, Chickpea, Apple, and Veggies Purée
Friday	**Breakfast:** 2–4 TB. oatmeal + 2 TB. Cranberry Apple Pear Purée **Lunch:** 2–4 TB. Quinoa, Chickpea, Apple, and Veggies Purée **Dinner:** 2–4 TB. beef and carrot purée + smashed white potato
Saturday	**Breakfast:** 2–4 TB. oatmeal + 2 TB. Cranberry Apple Pear Purée **Lunch:** 2–4 TB. beef and carrot purée + smashed white potato **Dinner:** 2–4 TB. Indian-Spiced Black Bean and Spinach Purée
Sunday	**Breakfast:** 2–4 TB. oatmeal + 2 TB. Cranberry Apple Pear Purée **Lunch:** 2–4 TB. Indian-Spiced Black Bean and Spinach Purée **Dinner:** 2–4 TB. beef and carrot purée + mashed potato

7 to 8 months

purées on the go

If you ever plan to leave your house for a meal with your little one, you may want to consider purchasing reusable or disposable pouches for your homemade purées.

These plastic pouches are easily available online and in some baby stores. They hold a few ounces of purée and have a screw cap on one end. Some little ones will have no trouble holding them and eating from them, while others may need assistance. Pouches are a great way to store purées in either the fridge or freezer.

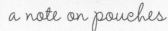

a note on pouches

Pouches should not replace meals at home, especially as baby begins eating less puréed food and more solids. It's important for kiddos to get used to chewing and the slower pace of regular eating. But when you're on the go and still want to feed your little one homemade goodness, then the pouch is the way to go.

Reusable Pouches

Reusable pouches are a great for small batches of purées and the occasional meal on the run. This style of pouch is made of sturdy, flexible plastic and generally has a zipper-lock opening for filling. My favorite kind has the opening on the bottom of the pouch. These pouches are great for single batches of purée or homemade yogurt blends. You can wash them in hot water with mild detergent and a bottlebrush. They generally last for three to six months, depending on how often you use them.

To fill reusable pouches:

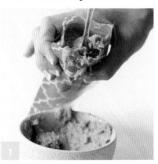

Spoon the purée through the opening (make sure the cap is on).

Seal the opening. Rinse off any drips of spilled purée, and you're good to go!

Disposable Pouches

Disposable pouches are made of thinner plastic and are intended to be discarded after one use. This style of pouch is great for large batches of purées and can be filled and stored easily, but they demand a little more investment than reusable pouches. Most brands of disposable pouches require a special tool for filling, often called a filling station. The filling station generally includes a system of tubes, plungers, and places to attach the bags. If you anticipate using pouches frequently, or if you appreciate the convenience of one-time-use pouches, you may want to invest in this style.

To fill disposable pouches:

Screw the pouches into the openings. Spoon some of the purée into the tube and use the plunger to push it into the bag. Repeat with remaining bags.

Remove the bags and attach the caps.

finger foods

Babies at this age are beginning to be able to feed themselves soft finger foods, such as noodles and steamed vegetables. Good finger foods for this age include the following:

steamed vegetables

Baby carrots

Sweet bell pepper strips

Broccoli

Green beans

Cauliflower

Fingerling potatoes

Sweet potato slices

Peas (from fresh or frozen)

Apple and pear slices (peel on)

fresh fruits and vegetables

Raw sweet bell pepper strips

Ripe mango strips

Under-ripe pineapple strips

Banana strips, quartered

Cucumber, grated and peeled

Diced avocado

grains

Cold whole-wheat spaghetti noodles

Hard breadsticks (great for teething)

Dry strips of whole-grain toast

proteins

Hard-boiled eggs

Thick slices of cheese

Steaming Finger Foods

The microwave is my preferred method for lightly steaming fruits and vegetables. It's fast and easy, and doesn't require a lot of cleanup. Use a fresh produce steamer, or put the produce in a glass bowl, add 2 tablespoons to ¼ cup water (depending on how much produce you are steaming), and cover with a small glass plate.

Carrots and Fingerling Potatoes

1. *Carrots:* Use baby carrots or peeled carrots cut into 2- to 3-inch (5–7.5cm) pieces. *Fingerling potatoes:* Scrub and leave whole.

2. Microwave on high for 8 to 10 minutes until tender.

Bell Pepper Strips

1. Wash and cut into ¼-inch (.5cm) strips.

2. Microwave on high for 1 to 2 minutes until soft.

Sweet Potato Slices

1. Wash and peel sweet potatoes. Slice into ¼-inch (.5cm) slices.

2. Microwave on high for 4 to 5 minutes.

Broccoli and Green Beans

1. *Broccoli:* Wash and cut into bite-size pieces, making sure there is enough stem for your little one to grab. *Green beans:* Wash and remove the ends.

2. Microwave on high for 2 to 2½ minutes.

Apple and Pear Slices

1. Wash and slice into ¼-inch (.5cm) slices.

2. Microwave on high for 3 to 4 minutes.

Cauliflower

1. Cut into bite-sized pieces, making sure there is enough of a stem for baby to hold onto.

2. Microwave on high for 3 to 4 minutes.

finger food safety

Although you should always let baby feed herself the finger foods, never leave a child unattended while feeding. In general, strips of food are better than chunks.

beets and berries *purée*

Beets are naturally sweet, but their taste can be a little overpowering for young palates. Pairing them with berries highlights their natural sweetness and creates a vibrantly hued purée.

PREP	5 minutes
YIELD	3 cups

1 cup strawberries, fresh or thawed from frozen

1 cup blueberries, fresh or thawed from frozen

1 cup cooked beets

1. Combine strawberries, blueberries, and beets in the blender and purée until it reaches the desired consistency.

2. Refrigerate in an airtight container for up to 1 week or store in the freezer for up to 3 months.

note
You can substitute mixed berries or frozen berry blends for the strawberries and blueberries.

preparing beets
My preferred method for preparing beets is to roast them. To roast beets: Preheat oven to 350°F (180°C). Scrub unpeeled beets and cut into 2- to 3-inch (5-7.5cm) slices. Toss with a bit of olive oil and fold into a foil packet. Place foil packet on a baking sheet and roast for 1 hour. When cool to the touch, rub off skins with a paper towel.

pumpkin berry patch *purée*

PREP	5 minutes
YIELD	1 cup

This is a sweet and easy purée to throw together. Pumpkin has fiber, potassium, and antioxidants. Its rich orange color is a sign that it's high in vitamin A, a nutrient essential for babies. The banana adds a little natural sweetness and the berries are a great source of vitamin C.

½ cup frozen mixed berries, thawed

¼ cup pure pumpkin purée

½ ripe banana

1. Combine all ingredients in the blender and purée until it reaches the desired consistency. Serve immediately.

2. Store leftovers in the fridge for up to 5 days or in the freezer for up to 3 months.

7 to 8 months

cherry, apple, and cloves *purée*

Cloves and cinnamon give this purée a wonderful aromatic spiciness. If the spices are too intense for your little one, try swirling it with plain whole-milk yogurt, or omit the ground cloves.

PREP	5 minutes
COOK	5 minutes
YIELD	1 cup

¼ cup dried apricots

½ cup hot water

1 organic apple, sliced

¾ cup frozen dark sweet cherries

Pinch ground cloves

¼ tsp. ground cinnamon

1. In a small bowl, cover dried apricots with hot water. Let sit for 2 minutes.

2. Place sliced apple in a glass bowl. Add 2 TB. water. Cover with a plate and microwave on high for 2 minutes.

3. Place apples, steaming water, apricots, cherries, ground cloves, and cinnamon in a blender. Purée until it reaches the desired consistency. Serve immediately.

4. Store leftovers in the fridge for up to 5 days or in the freezer for up to 3 months.

nutritional note

Dried apricots contain fiber, which can help baby stay regular. They also contain a small amount of iron, a mineral that your baby needs more of at around 6 months.

7 to 8 months

cranberry apple pear *purée*

PREP	5 minutes
COOK	3 to 4 hours
YIELD	3 cups
SPECIAL TOOLS	slow cooker

This pink purée is packed with flavor. It's the perfect balance between sweet and tart. We tend to think of sweet as the only flavor that babies will like, but tart is an important flavor, too. If we never give it to them, how will they like it? For older kiddos, this is great swirled with yogurt or served with turkey or pork.

1 cup cranberries, fresh or frozen

3 small apples or 2 medium apples, sliced and skin-on

2 small pears or 1 large pear, sliced and skin-on

½ cup raisins

½ cup water

3 cinnamon sticks

1. Combine all ingredients in a medium slow cooker. Cook on low for 3 to 4 hours until you can easily pierce the fruit with a fork. Remove cinnamon sticks.

2. Transfer mixture to a blender. Purée until it reaches the desired consistency. Refrigerate in an airtight container for up to 1 week or store in the freezer for up to 3 months.

nutritional note

Cranberries are nutritional powerhouses! They are loaded with antioxidants, and can help prevent infections in baby's digestive tract and urinary system. They are a perfect food to include if you want to boost your baby's immunity.

apple, carrots, greens, and beans *purée*

PREP	5 minutes
COOK	10 minutes
YIELD	3 cups

This is a complete meal in a purée. It's great for filling your pouches and keeping on hand for on-the-go meals. Feel free to substitute kale for the spinach, pears for the apples, black beans for chickpeas, and parsnips or sweet potatoes for the carrots. In short, you can make this recipe your own!

2 medium apples

2 medium carrots

1 to 1 1/2 cups water

2 cups spinach

1 cup chickpeas, rinsed and drained

1. Cut apples into 1-inch (2.5cm) slices. Cut carrots in 2-inch (5cm) slices.

2. Place apples and carrots in the steaming basket of a microwave steamer. Pour 1 to 1 1/2 cups water into the steaming base. Microwave on high for 6 minutes.

3. Add spinach and microwave on high for 1 to 2 minutes until spinach is wilted and carrots and apples are fork-tender. Reserve steaming water.

4. Combine apples, carrots, spinach, 1 cup steaming water, and chickpeas in a blender. Purée until it reaches the desired consistency.

5. Store leftovers in the fridge for up to 5 days or in the freezer for up to 3 months.

kale, apple, and sweet potato *purée*

I love healthy food, and even I struggle with kale. It can be tough and bitter on its own, but it's a powerhouse in the world of vegetables. Just one cup of kale provides 100 percent of our vitamin A, C, and K needs. Even though this recipe is packed with kale, all your baby will taste is the sweetness from the apple and sweet potato.

PREP	5 minutes
COOK	8 to 10 minutes
YIELD	1 cup

½ large sweet potato or 1 small sweet potato

1 medium apple

¼ to ½ cup water

2 generous handfuls kale, stems removed, approximately 2 cups

¼ tsp. ground nutmeg

1. Slice sweet potato and apple into ¼-inch (.5cm) slices.

2. Place apple and sweet potato in the steaming basket of a microwave steamer. Pour ¼ cup to ½ cup water into the base. Microwave on high for 6 minutes, until fork-tender.

3. Add kale and microwave on high for 2 minutes. Reserve steaming water.

4. Combine sweet potato, apple, kale, ground nutmeg, and ¼ cup to ½ cup steaming water in a blender. Purée until it reaches the desired consistency.

5. Store in a covered container in the fridge for 3 days or in the freezer for up to 3 months.

chicken, kale, and sweet potato *purée*

PREP	10 minutes
COOK	10 minutes
YIELD	2 cups

This is a great purée for using up leftover chicken and introducing meat to baby's diet. It packs a nutritional punch, too. It's rich in vitamin K, vitamin A, iron, and antioxidants, all of which are important for a growing baby.

1 medium sweet potato, scrubbed and ends removed, sliced into ¼-inch (.5cm) slices (approximately 1 cup)

1 cup chopped kale, packed

1 cup cooked chicken

¼ tsp. ground nutmeg

1 to 1½ cups water

1. Place sweet potato in a fresh produce microwave steamer with 1 to 1½ cups water. Microwave on high for 6 minutes.

2. Add kale and microwave for an additional 2 minutes or until kale is cooked and sweet potatoes are fork-tender. Reserve 1 cup steaming water.

2. Combine sweet potato, kale, chicken, nutmeg, and ¾ cup steaming water in the blender. Purée until smooth, adding more reserved steaming water if needed. Serve immediately.

3. Refrigerate in an airtight container for up to 5 days or in the freezer for up to 3 months.

quinoa, chickpea, apple, and veggies *purée*

PREP	5 minutes
COOK	10 minutes
YIELD	3 cups

This purée provides all the elements of a complete meal. I love taking these types of purées on outings because I know as long as my little one eats the purée, she is getting a balanced meal. I whip it up whenever I have leftover quinoa.

2 medium apples

2 medium carrots or parsnips

1 to 1½ cups water

1 cup cooked quinoa

1 cup chickpeas, rinsed and drained

¼ tsp. ground nutmeg

1. Cut apples into 1-inch (2.5cm) slices. Cut carrots in 2-inch (5cm) slices.

2. Place apples and carrots in the steaming basket of a microwave steamer. Pour 1 to 1½ cups water into the steaming base. Microwave on high for 7 to 8 minutes, until carrots and apples are fork-tender. Reserve steaming water.

3. Combine apples, carrots, 1 cup steaming water, quinoa, chickpeas, and nutmeg in a blender. Purée until it reaches the desired consistency.

4. Store leftovers in the fridge for up to 5 days or in the freezer for up to 3 months.

hard-boiled *eggs*

Hard-boiled eggs can be a great introduction to eggs for kiddos. You can slice them, mash them, or just cut them in half. Their soft texture is easy for little mouths to break down, and it's a convenient protein to keep on hand for quick meals or snacks. Although the recipe calls for a full dozen eggs, you can use the same method with fewer eggs if needed.

PREP	5 minutes
COOK	25 minutes
YIELD	1 dozen eggs
SERVING SIZE	1 egg

12 eggs	1 TB. white vinegar	1 TB. salt

1. Place eggs in a large saucepan. Cover with cool water. Add salt and vinegar. Gently stir to dissolve.

2. Bring to a rolling boil over high heat. Let boil for 1 minute. Cover and remove from heat. Let eggs sit in hot water for 20 minutes.

3. While eggs cook, prepare a large bowl of ice and water. When eggs are done, transfer them to the ice bath. Keep eggs in bath until they are cool to the touch (replace ice if necessary).

4. Refrigerate eggs in an airtight container for up to 5 days.

egg-peeling tips

- Use older eggs. Younger, fresher eggs will be harder to peel.

- Bring eggs to room temperature before peeling.

- Gently rap the egg against the counter to break the shell. Then gently roll the egg under your hand to loosen the shell from the egg.

- Peel the egg under running water.

indian-spiced black bean and spinach purée

Garam masala is an aromatic Indian spice blend that includes sweet cinnamon and savory cumin along with several other spices. Because it has sweet and savory elements, it makes a great gateway spice for baby. In this purée, the bitterness of the spinach is offset by the sweet potato, and the beans add protein and fiber.

PREP	5 minutes
COOK	10 minutes
YIELD	2 cups

1 medium sweet potato, scrubbed and ends removed, sliced into 1/4-inch (.5cm) slices (approximately 1 cup)

1 cup water

1 cup frozen organic spinach

1 cup black beans, rinsed and drained

1/4 tsp. garam masala

1. Place sweet potato in a fresh produce microwave steamer with 1 cup water. Microwave on high for 6 minutes.

2. Add frozen spinach and microwave for 1 minute more or until spinach is cooked and sweet potatoes are fork-tender. Reserve 1/2 cup steaming water.

3. Combine sweet potatoes, spinach, beans, garam masala, and 1/2 cup steaming water in the blender and purée until smooth.

4. Refrigerate in an airtight container for up to 5 days or in the freezer for up to 3 months.

garam masala

You can make your own garam masala with spices you already have in your pantry. Combine 1 1/2 TB. cinnamon, 1 TB. cumin, 1 TB. coriander, 2 tsp. ground black pepper, 2 tsp. ground cloves, 1 1/2 tsp. nutmeg, and 1/2 tsp. ground ginger. Mix well and store in an airtight container away from light.

part 4

9 to 11 months

At 9 to 11 months, your kiddo's eating skills have made
big improvements. He's getting better at picking up
small pieces of food, and it's easier for him to control
food in his mouth. With these new skills, it's the perfect
time to let him practice with more lumps and bumps.
This section focuses on chunkier foods for baby. You'll
find recipes for soups, creamy combinations like egg
salad, and new options for finger foods like baby
biscotti and roasted carrots.

what baby is eating now: *chunkier foods*

Now's the time to bridge the gap between purées and table food. This just means you give your baby food that has more lumps and bumps. Baby needs to get more practice with chewing before he can progress to toddler foods. Plus, he needs to know that food isn't always silky-smooth like a purée.

Instead of puréeing all of baby's meals, try to finely chop, grind, or lightly blend his foods. The goal is to leave some chunks for baby to chew. You can still give baby some of his favorite purées; just make sure that the majority of his meals have a chunkier consistency.

Chunky Foods to Try

- Soups, stews, and chili
- Fresh, ripe berries (smashed or cut into pieces)
- Steel-cut oatmeal or old-fashioned oatmeal
- Finely ground meats or shreds of pulled chicken or pork
- Flakes of fresh cooked fish
- Egg salad and chicken salad
- Creamy noodle or rice dishes (cut up large or long noodles)
- Soft chunks of tofu
- Pieces of soft breads and muffins
- Scrambled eggs
- Strips of roasted carrots

Make the Transition Easy

When introducing chunkier foods to baby (especially meat), it can be helpful if the food is moistened with a sauce or broth. Soups and stews are a great place to start. Slow cookers are wonderful for making soft meals that are perfect for baby—and easier on you!

New Capabilities

During this stage, baby starts to develop what's known as the "pincer grasp." Instead of picking things up with his palm, he starts to use his thumb and forefinger. With this new skill, he will become more active at feeding himself (if he hasn't already). Make sure to give him lots of opportunities to practice picking food up from his tray.

What About Snacks?

Baby is eating three solid meals per day with breast milk or formula in between. Right now, snacks aren't necessary. Snacks start when baby is weaned, and when he becomes more physically active.

nutritional needs: 9 to 11 *months*

At 9 to 11 months, baby continues to grow at the same pace. You should expect to see him gain 3 to 5 ounces (80–140g) per week, or about 1 pound (450g) per month. Breast milk or formula is still the bulk of baby's diet, with 3 to 4 feedings per day, or 24 to 30 ounces (710–950ml).

Now that baby's almost 1 year old, he should be working on eating a greater variety of foods and textures. You may also see him eating a bit more at his meals. Here are approximate serving sizes for baby at this stage.

Fruits: ¼ cup per day

Vegetables: ¼ cup per day

Whole grains: ½ to ¾ cup per day

Meat and protein-rich foods: 2 to 3 tablespoons per day

Nutritional Spotlight: Omega-3 Fatty Acids

Omega-3 fatty acids are a type of healthy fat that our bodies do not produce naturally. In children, omega-3 fatty acids are crucial to brain and eye health. During the first two years of life, your baby's brain will have a giant growth spurt. To support and nurture this growth, it's wise to get him eating omega-3s early on. In a study done at Oxford University, published in the journal *PLOS ONE*, children with higher blood levels of omega-3s performed better in school and had fewer behavioral problems.

Omega-3 fats are found in high concentrations in certain fish and seafood, but they are also found in some plant foods. The form found in fish and seafood seems to be the most easily absorbed by the body.

RECIPE TO TRY: Roasted Salmon

foods rich in omega-3s

Wild Alaskan salmon: Fork into flakes for baby to pick up, or make small salmon patties.

Walnuts: Grind in a food processor to a sandy consistency. Add to applesauce, fruit purees, mashed bananas, yogurt, oatmeal, and baked goods.

Chia seed and flaxseed: Add a tiny pinch to fruit purées, yogurt, applesauce, mashed bananas, oatmeal, baked goods, and smoothies. Flax must be ground in order to get the benefits.

Omega-3 eggs: Try scrambled or hard-boiled and chop into pieces for finger food.

meal plans:
9 to 11 months

Here are daily and weekly meal plans for feeding your little one at this stage. Keep in mind that every baby is different. This is only meant to be a guide, not a strict schedule.

Sample Feeding Schedule

TIME	SLEEP AND FOOD
6:00–7:00 AM	Baby wakes and is nursed or bottle-fed.
7:30–8:00 AM	Breakfast: protein (yogurt, egg) + fruit **or** oatmeal + fruit
9:00 AM	Baby naps for 1 hour.
10:00 AM	Baby is nursed or bottle-fed.
11:30 AM	Lunch: protein + veggie + starch or fruit
1:00 PM	Baby naps 1 to 2 hours.
2:00–3:00 PM	Baby wakes and is nursed or bottle-fed.
5:00–6:00 PM	Dinner: protein + veggie + starch or fruit
7:00–7:30 PM	Nurse or bottle-feed before bed.

Meal Key

Protein = meat, beans, lentils, yogurt, and cheese

Starch = whole grains, potatoes, peas, winter squash (butternut, acorn), and corn

Veggie = any vegetable other than peas, potatoes, winter squash, or corn

notes

- Serving sizes are estimated to give you an idea of what a balanced meal looks like at this stage. It's completely normal if your child refuses one food and instead eats more of something else. Don't stress so much about serving sizes, but rather focus on providing healthy food.

- Since baby is older, this meal plan emphasizes finger foods. If baby is still into purées, feel free to include some in his meal plan.

- Three different breakfasts are rotated in this plan to show you options. Feel free to offer the same breakfast each day if that's what you want to do.

Sample Weekly Meal Plan

DAY	MEALS
Monday	**Breakfast:** Banana Egg Pancake, cut into pieces **Lunch:** 1–2 TB. cooked black beans + 1 TB. cheese strips + 2 TB. avocado chunks **Dinner:** Italian Meatball + 2–4 TB. spaghetti squash + 2–4 TB. steamed broccoli chunks
Tuesday	**Breakfast:** 2–4 TB. Homemade Yogurt + 2 TB. mashed fresh strawberries **Lunch:** LO Italian Meatball + 2–4 TB. spaghetti squash + 2 TB. steamed broccoli chunks **Dinner:** ¼–½ cup Veggie Curry
Wednesday	**Breakfast:** ¼ cup Instant Oatmeal + 2 TB. mashed banana **Lunch:** ¼–½ cup LO Veggie Curry **Dinner:** 2 TB. Roasted Salmon flakes + 2 TB. steamed green peas + 2 TB. applesauce
Thursday	**Breakfast:** Banana Egg Pancake, cut into pieces **Lunch:** 1–2 TB. Tofu Bites + 2 TB. LO peas + 2 TB. applesauce **Dinner:** ¼–½ cup Chicken Noodle Soup
Friday	**Breakfast:** 2–4 TB. Homemade Yogurt + 2 TB. mashed fresh strawberry **Lunch:** ¼–½ cup LO Chicken Noodle Soup **Dinner:** ½ cup Asian Ground Pork + 2 TB. Coconut Rice
Saturday	**Breakfast:** ¼ cup Instant Oatmeal + 2 TB. applesauce **Lunch:** ¼–½ cup LO Chicken Noodle Soup **Dinner:** ½ cup LO Asian Ground Pork + 2 TB. LO Coconut Rice
Sunday	**Breakfast:** 2–4 TB. Homemade Yogurt + 2 TB. mashed banana **Lunch:** ¼ cup Egg Salad + 2 TB. steamed broccoli chunks **Dinner:** 1–2 TB. LO Tofu Bites + 2–4 TB. Creamy Noodles + 2 TB. steamed carrots

*LO = leftover

easy freezer *meals*

PREP	20 minutes
COOK	40 minutes
YIELD	6 bags or 12 meals
SERVING SIZE	½ bag
SPECIAL TOOLS	6 quart-size zipper-lock bags

note

Make sure to use fresh chicken (not thawed from frozen). Refreezing chicken will affect the taste and texture. You can swap the quinoa for another cooked grain, such as rice or couscous.

The idea for these meals came from a friend in my daughter's playgroup, Kinsey Schultz, who felt she could easily replicate store-bought frozen baby meals at home. I thought she was a genius and ran with the idea. In just an hour, you can prep 12 meals for your little one. And if your kiddo goes through a "no-food-can-touch" phase, you can serve these on a bed of greens for a healthy and tasty adult meal.

2 cups water

1 quart (1l) vegetable broth

3 cloves garlic, peeled and smashed

2 bay leaves

1 medium onion, peeled and quartered

4 (4-oz.; 110g) boneless, skinless chicken breasts

1 cup uncooked quinoa

1 (16-oz.; 450g) bag frozen mixed vegetables

Seasonings of your choice

1. *Poach the chicken:* Combine water, 2 cups vegetable broth, garlic, bay leaves, and onion in a large saucepan. Bring to a boil over high heat. Add chicken and fully submerge (you may need to add additional water). Bring to a boil. Cover and reduce heat to medium-low. Simmer for 15 minutes. Remove from heat and let chicken sit for 5 minutes. Remove and cut chicken into small pieces.

2. *Cook the quinoa:* Combine quinoa with 2 cups water in a medium saucepan. Bring to a boil. Cover and reduce heat to low. Simmer for 10 minutes. Fluff with a fork and remove from heat.

3. *Cook the vegetables:* Place vegetables in microwave-safe dish. Add 2 tablespoons water, cover, and microwave for 3 minutes on high. Stir. Microwave for an additional 6 minutes.

4. *Assemble the bags:* For easy filling, place a zipper-lock bag in a drinking glass and fold the edges over the rim. In each zipper-lock bag, place ⅓ cup poached chicken, ⅓ cup cooked vegetables, ¼ cup cooked quinoa, 1 tsp. seasoning of your choice, and ¼ cup vegetable broth. Make sure to label each bag!

5. *Freeze the bags:* Press all of the air out of the bag and lay it flat. Store in the fridge overnight and then transfer to the freezer.

6. *Thaw as needed:* To use, thaw in the fridge or in a bowl of cool water. Microwave for 15 to 20 seconds to bring contents of bag to room temperature or slightly warmer. Do not refreeze leftovers.

seasoning suggestions

This is a great place to use seasoning blends (such as Italian, Greek, or Asian) that you may have in your pantry.

Here are some other suggestions:

- **BBQ:** Smoked paprika
- **Indian:** Curry or garam masala
- **Mexican:** Cumin
- **Italian:** Oregano or basil, or both

jam-filled *breakfast muffins*

PREP	25 minutes
COOK	15 to 20 minutes for mini muffins; 18 to 25 minutes for regular muffins
YIELD	24 mini muffins or 12 regular muffins
SERVING SIZE	2 mini muffins or 1 regular muffin

note

If you can't find whole-wheat pastry flour, use all-purpose flour. Don't substitute white whole-wheat flour or whole-wheat flour in this recipe.

These are a great breakfast treat for your little one: nutty whole grains coupled with the sweetness of jam. I love making a batch and throwing them in the freezer so they last longer. Mini muffins are the perfect size for little hands, but if you don't have a mini muffin pan, you can use a regular muffin pan with great results.

3 cups whole-wheat pastry flour

1/2 cup quick-cooking oats

1 1/2 tsp. baking soda

1 tsp. ground cinnamon

1/8 tsp. salt

1/2 cup butter, softened

1/2 cup brown sugar, packed

1/2 cup unsweetened applesauce

1 tsp. vanilla extract

3/4 to 1 cup jam of your choice

1. Preheat oven to 350°F (180°C). Grease a 24-cup mini muffin pan (or a 12-cup regular muffin pan).

2. In a medium bowl, whisk together whole-wheat pastry flour, oats, baking soda, cinnamon, and salt.

3. In a large bowl, use an electric mixer to cream together butter, sugar, applesauce, and vanilla extract. Reduce speed to low and add flour mixture. You may need to use a wooden spoon or your hands to get it all combined.

4. Use a small cookie scoop to scoop dough into muffin pan (approx. 1/2 TB. dough). Flatten dough into pan. Add 1 tsp. jam to each cup.

5. Scoop another 1/2 TB. dough on top of the jam. Then flatten into a disc and seal the edges.

6. Bake 15 to 20 minutes (18 to 25 minutes for regular muffins) until tops are golden and starting to crack. Let cool to room temperature before storing.

7. Store in an airtight container at room temperature for 3 to 5 days, in the fridge for up to 1 week, or in the freezer for up to 2 months. To thaw, allow to sit at room temperature for 30 to 60 minutes, or heat in microwave for 15 to 20 seconds. Let cool before you give it to your kiddo as the jam may get hot.

Press dough into pan and top with jam (step 4).

Place a dough "lid" over the jam and seal the edges (step 5).

banana egg *pancake*

PREP	5 minutes
COOK	10 minutes
YIELD	1 pancake
SERVING SIZE	1 pancake

This recipe was my gateway to get Baby G to eat eggs. The sweetness of the banana masks the egg flavor, and it is a great way to use ripe bananas. Rather than using syrup, I add cinnamon and vanilla so no toppings are needed. If your baby likes a little added sweetness, try topping with unsweetened applesauce.

½ ripe banana

1 large egg

¼ tsp. ground cinnamon

½ tsp. vanilla extract

note

You can easily double this recipe and cook in a medium 10-inch (25cm) frying pan.

1. In a small bowl, mash banana with a fork. Add egg, cinnamon, and vanilla. Whisk until combined.

2. Heat a 7- or 8-inch (17–20cm) frying pan over medium heat. Spray with cooking spray or add butter to grease.

3. Pour in batter, making sure it covers the whole pan. Cook for 5 to 7 minutes, until bottom is set and starting to turn golden brown. Flip and cook for an additional 2 to 3 minutes until pancake is cooked through. Serve immediately.

9 to 11 months

instant oatmeal

In just 15 minutes, you can make almost two weeks' worth of instant oatmeal with your own ingredients. The texture is the same as store-bought instant oatmeal, making it an easy transition for your kids. Unlike store-bought packets, however, the taste isn't overwhelmed with sweetness, and the cinnamon and dried fruit really shine.

PREP	15 minutes
COOK	2 minutes
YIELD	12 to 13 bags
SERVING SIZE	1 bag
SPECIAL TOOLS	13 snack-size zipper-lock bags

2 cups quick-cooking oats

1/3 cup powdered nonfat milk

1/4 tsp. salt

1 1/2 tsp. ground cinnamon

1/2 tsp. ground nutmeg

1/3 cup brown sugar, packed

1 1/4 cup unsweetened dried fruit (dried cranberries, blueberries, apricots, figs, and/or raisins)

1. In a large bowl, mix together oats, powdered milk, salt, cinnamon, nutmeg, and brown sugar. Add dried fruit and stir to combine.

2. Scoop 1/3 cup of mixture into each zipper-lock bag. Store the bags in a large glass jar or a gallon-size zipper-lock bag.

3. To make oatmeal, place the contents of one bag in a small bowl and stir in 1/3 to 1/2 cup water. Microwave on high for 1 minute and let sit for 1 minute. Serve immediately.

variation

To make **Dairy-Free Instant Oatmeal,** take out the powdered nonfat milk. Pulse 1/3 cup instant oats in a blender until it forms a fine powder. Substitute the oat powder for the powdered milk.

flavorful and fun yogurt ideas

Fruit Yogurt: Mix ½ cup yogurt with ½ to 1 tsp. fruit spread.

Frozen Yogurt Bites: Line a tray with wax paper and squeeze dime-sized dots of yogurt from a reusable pouch onto the tray. Freeze for 3 to 4 hours. It's a great treat for teethers!

Vanilla Yogurt: Mix ½ cup yogurt with ¼ tsp. vanilla extract. Add more to taste.

Sweetened Yogurt with Fruit: Mix ½ cup yogurt with ¼ tsp. real maple syrup and chopped fruit.

Granola and Yogurt: Add a handful of granola to ½ cup yogurt. Great for little ones who are just starting to feed themselves.

Citrus Zest Yogurt: Stir in ¼ tsp. honey and zest from an orange or grapefruit.

Sour Cream: Swap Greek Yogurt for sour cream on tacos, enchiladas, or baked potatoes.

homemade yogurt

Making your own yogurt is much easier than you might think. It just takes a little time at the stove and a night in the oven, and you have 8 cups of homemade creamy goodness.

½ gallon (2l) organic whole milk

¼ cup organic plain yogurt

PREP	5 minutes
COOK	10 hours
YIELD	8 cups
SERVING SIZE	½ cup
SPECIAL TOOLS	digital meat or candy thermometer

1. Place a 3-quart (3l) or larger glass or ceramic covered casserole dish (or any glass container with a cover) on a cooling rack.

2. Pour ¼ cup milk into a small bowl and set aside. Pour remaining milk into a heavy-bottomed pot over medium-high heat.

3. Heat milk over medium-high heat until a digital thermometer reads 180°F (82°C), approximately 10 to 15 minutes. Stir often with wooden spoon so that milk does not scorch.

4. Pour hot milk into casserole dish and let cool to 105° to 110°F (40° to 43°C), approximately 45 minutes to 1 hour.

5. While milk is cooling, whisk together yogurt and reserved milk and preheat oven to 200°F (93°C).

6. Once the milk has cooled, stir in the yogurt and milk mixture until well combined. Turn the oven off.

7. Cover casserole dish with lid and wrap it in two dishtowels so the dish is completely covered.

8. Place in warm oven and turn on oven light. Leave in oven for 8 to 9 hours. Do not open the oven door during this time.

9. After 8 to 9 hours, check on yogurt. It should be thick and creamy with some liquid on top. If it has not reached the desired consistency, return to oven for an additional hour.

10. Transfer yogurt to an airtight container (or individual airtight containers) and refrigerate for up to 3 weeks.

variations

To make **Greek Yogurt,** strain the yogurt by placing two layers of cheesecloth in a mesh strainer set inside a large bowl. Put the yogurt in the strainer and cover loosely with plastic wrap. Let sit for 2 to 4 hours until it reaches the desired consistency. Drain the liquid after the first hour.

To make **Yogurt Cheese**, strain the yogurt for 1 to 2 days.

9 to 11 months

whole-wheat sandwich bread

PREP	25 minutes
COOK	90 minutes (including rising)
YIELD	2 (9×5×3-in.; 23×12.5×7.5-cm) loaves
SERVING SIZE	¼ slice
SPECIAL TOOLS	stand mixer

This bread is reason enough to invest in a stand mixer. The mixer does all the work, and you can claim all the credit for this amazing sandwich bread that enables you to avoid the chemicals, unnecessary ingredients, and possible honey in store-bought bread. *(Recipe adapted from An Oregon Cottage blog, anoregoncottage.com.)*

3 cups bread flour	1½ TB. active yeast	⅓ cup maple syrup
3 cups whole-wheat flour	⅓ cup mild oil (grapeseed oil or canola oil)	2½ tsp. salt
2 cups warm water		

1. Grease 2 standard (9×5×3-in.; 23×12.5×7.5-cm) loaf pans with oil spray.

2. In the mixer bowl of a stand mixer, combine 1 cup bread flour, 1 cup whole-wheat flour, water, and yeast. Let sit for 15 minutes.

3. Add remaining 2 cups bread flour, 2 cups whole-wheat flour, oil, maple syrup, and salt. Put the oil in the measuring cup before the syrup and you won't leave any syrup in the cup. Stir to combine.

4. Fit mixer with dough hook and begin mixing on medium-low speed. Dough will begin to clump after 1 to 2 minutes. When the dough begins to pull away from the sides of the bowl, continue mixing on medium-low for 6 to 7 minutes.

5. Divide the dough in half. Shape one half into a loaf and place in prepared pan. Repeat with other half of dough.

6. Let rise for 60 minutes in a warm place. With 10 minutes remaining on your rise, preheat the oven to 350°F (180°C). Bake for 30 minutes, rotating halfway through the baking time.

7. Let cool for 10 minutes on a wire rack. Slide a butter knife around the edges of the pan to loosen the loaf. Invert onto rack and cool completely.

8. Store wrapped in plastic wrap for 2 days at room temperature. To freeze, wrap in plastic wrap and foil, and place in a zipper-lock freezer bag. Store frozen for up to 2 months.

tip

If you use an oven with a warm setting (200°F; 93°C) to rise the bread, cut the rise time to 45 minutes and leave the bread in the oven while it preheats.

whole-wheat bis-sticks

These bis-sticks are somewhere between a flaky biscuit and a doughy breadstick. They're super easy to make and super tasty for dunking into soups, gravies, and sauces. The mild flavor and soft texture are great for little ones.

PREP	10 minutes
COOK	16 to 20 minutes
YIELD	12 bis-sticks
SERVING SIZE	1 bis-stick

3 cups whole-wheat pastry flour

1 TB. baking powder

2 TB. sugar

1 tsp. garlic salt

2 tsp. dried basil

1/4 cup Parmesan cheese, grated

1 cup whole milk

1/2 cup olive oil

1. Preheat the oven to 425°F (220°C).

2. In a large bowl, combine flour, baking powder, sugar, garlic salt, basil, and cheese. Add milk and 1/4 cup olive oil. Stir until dough is formed. Use your hands to knead the dough in the bowl until smooth.

3. Pour the remaining 1/4 cup olive oil into a 10×15–inch (25×38cm) cake pan. Place dough in pan and press to cover the bottom of the pan. Flip the dough over so that there is oil on both sides and press to edges again.

4. Using a pizza cutter, cut dough into 2-inch (5cm) strips. Bake for 16 to 20 minutes, until golden brown and cooked through.

5. Serve immediately. You may need to re-cut the strips after they come out of the oven. Store leftovers in a zipper-lock bag for 2 to 3 days at room temperature, or for up to 5 days in the fridge.

variation

To make **Cinnamon Raisin Bis-sticks,** substitute melted butter for oil. Omit cheese, basil, and garlic salt. Add 2 additional TB. sugar (making the total 1/4 cup), 1 TB. ground cinnamon, 1/2 cup raisins, and 1/4 tsp. salt. Top with a sweet glaze by whisking together 2 cups powdered sugar, 2 TB. melted butter, 2 TB. whole milk, and 1 tsp. vanilla.

9 to 11 months

whole-grain cornbread

PREP	10 minutes
COOK	25 to 30 minutes for pan; 20 to 25 minutes for muffins
YIELD	1 (8×8-inch; 20×20cm) pan or 12 muffins
SERVING SIZE	1 piece or ½ muffin

This whole-grain bread is perfect for eating with chili, soup, barbecue chicken, or just as a great afternoon snack. I based this recipe on a King Arthur Flour recipe. The sweetness from the corn makes it an appealing dinnertime bread for little ones.

1¼ cup milk, room temperature

2 tsp. apple cider vinegar

1¾ cups whole-wheat pastry flour

1 cup yellow cornmeal, finely ground

¼ cup sugar

2 tsp. baking powder

¼ tsp. baking soda

¼ tsp. salt

1 cup yellow corn, fresh or frozen

¼ cup butter, melted and cooled

¼ cup mild oil (such as grapeseed or canola)

1 large egg, room temperature

1. Preheat oven to 375°F (190°C). Grease an 8×8-inch (20×20cm) cake pan or a 12-cup muffin pan with softened butter.

2. In a liquid measuring cup, combine milk and apple cider vinegar.

3. In a large bowl, whisk together whole-wheat pastry flour, cornmeal, sugar, baking powder, baking soda, and salt. Add corn and stir to combine.

4. In a medium bowl, combine milk mixture, butter, oil, and egg.

5. Mix wet ingredients into dry ingredients. Stir just until combined. Pour batter into prepared pan.

6. For an 8×8-inch (20×20cm) pan, bake for 25 to 30 minutes or until sides are pulling away from the pan and a toothpick inserted in the middle comes out with just a few crumbs on it. For muffins, bake 20 to 25 minutes or until a toothpick inserted in a muffin comes out with just a few crumbs.

7. Cool in pan on a cooling rack. When cool, cut into 2×2-inch (5×5cm) pieces. Store covered in the fridge for up to 7 days. Muffins can be frozen in a zipper-lock bag for up to 3 months.

creamy broccoli noodles

PREP	5 minutes
COOK	20 minutes
YIELD	3 to 4 cups
SERVING SIZE	½ cup

Pasta Alfredo is tricky to make when you have a toddler. There are multiple pans to watch and you have to stir the sauce just right or it breaks. As I learned one night, it's a recipe for disaster. Consider this a poor man's pasta Alfredo: all the great taste, none of the stress. Because you cook the broccoli with the pasta, it breaks down and creates a creamy broccoli sauce to coat your noodles.

2 to 4 oz. (55–110g) dry pasta

2 cups precut broccoli

1 cup frozen peas

½ medium red pepper, diced

½ cup whole milk

1 TB. whole-wheat pastry flour

Pinch ground white pepper

Pinch ground nutmeg

½ tsp. salt

2 TB. butter

½ cup shredded Parmesan cheese

1. Fill a large saucepan halfway with salted water and bring to a boil over high heat. Add pasta and broccoli. Simmer for 2 minutes less than directed, about 6 minutes. Add peas and red pepper. Cook an additional 2 minutes until pasta is tender.

2. Meanwhile, in a large liquid measuring cup, whisk together milk, flour, white pepper, and nutmeg.

3. Drain pasta. Return to pan and turn off the burner. Add butter, milk mixture, and cheese. Stir until butter and cheese are melted. Serve immediately.

4. Store leftovers in the fridge for up to 5 days.

tip

Look for bags of precut broccoli to cut down on prep time. If you can't find precut broccoli, add 5 to 10 minutes to your prep time.

veggie curry

This is a great recipe for introducing lots of veggies to your little one. Combining garam masala with cumin, turmeric, and chili powder creates a curry-like taste that's less pungent than most traditional curries. This makes a huge batch, but it freezes well and makes great leftovers.

PREP	25 to 35 minutes
COOK	8 to 10 hours
YIELD	12 cups
SERVING SIZE	½ cup
SPECIAL TOOLS	slow cooker

1 medium onion, diced

3 ribs celery, diced

1 medium sweet potato, peeled and diced

2 medium apples, peeled and diced

1 medium yellow squash, diced

1 medium red pepper, diced

2 cups baby carrots or precut carrot chips

1 cup precut cauliflower

2 cups green beans, frozen

2 (15-oz. 425g) cans chickpeas, rinsed and drained

3 cups vegetable broth

2 TB. garam masala

1 TB. turmeric

1 TB. cumin

½ TB. chili powder

2 cups fresh spinach

2 (14.5-oz; 411g) cans diced tomatoes, juices drained

1 cup light coconut milk

¼ tsp. salt

¼ tsp. ground black pepper

1. In a large slow cooker, combine onion, celery, sweet potato, apple, yellow squash, red pepper, carrots, cauliflower, green beans, and chickpeas.

2. In a medium bowl, whisk broth with garam masala, turmeric, cumin, and chili powder. Pour over vegetables in slow cooker. Cook on low for 8 to 10 hours.

3. Add spinach, tomatoes, and coconut milk 30 minutes before you are ready to eat. Season with salt and pepper. Adjust spices as needed. Serve with brown rice and naan bread.

4. Refrigerate for up to 5 days or store in the freezer for up to 3 months.

tip

Make a protein-packed grilled cheese by draining the liquid from a spoonful of leftover veggie curry and using it as a filling in a grilled cheese sandwich or quesadilla.

9 to 11 months

coconut rice

Use any leftover coconut milk and broth to make coconut rice. In a large saucepan, combine 1 cup coconut milk, 1 cup broth, 1 tsp. sugar, juice from 1 lime, and 1 cup dry brown rice. Bring to a boil and then reduce heat. Simmer for 30 to 40 minutes, stirring occasionally. You may need to add additional water as it cooks. This makes a great base for your curry!

roasted baby carrots

This is a great finger food for your little one because roasting the carrots makes them soft enough to gum. Roasting also brings out the natural sweetness of the carrots, which is heightened by the spiciness and saltiness of the seasonings.

PREP	5 minutes
COOK	30 to 45 minutes
YIELD	2 cups
SERVING SIZE	3 to 4 carrots

2 cups baby carrots

1 TB. grapeseed or olive oil

½ tsp. cumin

¼ tsp. chili powder

¼ tsp. salt

1. Preheat oven to 450°F (230°C). Line a rimmed baking sheet with parchment paper.

2. Place baby carrots on prepared pan. Drizzle with oil and sprinkle with cumin, chili powder, and salt. Shake to evenly spread spices.

3. Roast for 30 to 45 minutes until carrots are fork-tender and starting to crisp on outside. Smaller carrots will cook faster. Serve when cool enough for your little one.

4. Refrigerate in an airtight container for up to 3 days.

nutritional note

Carrots are rich in beta-carotene, a provitamin that is converted to vitamin A by the liver. Beta-carotene also has antioxidant properties that help protect against cancer and heart disease. Cooking actually boosts the amount of beta-carotene in carrots, making the nutrient more available to the body.

tofu *bites*

PREP	20 minutes
COOK	20 to 25 minutes
YIELD	24 to 28 rectangles
SERVING SIZE	2 to 3 rectangles

These little nuggets are just the right size for small hands to dunk in ketchup. The taste and texture are similar to chicken nuggets. This recipe makes a lot of bites, so I suggest mixing together the wheat germ and garlic powder and just making as many tofu bites as you would like. They make good leftovers, so prepare enough for two meals for you and your little one.

1 (10-oz.; 285g) package firm tofu

¼ cup wheat germ

1 tsp. garlic powder

1. Preheat oven to 425°F (220°C). Lightly spray a baking sheet with oil spray.

2. Cut tofu into small, bite-size rectangles.

3. In a small bowl, whisk together wheat germ and garlic powder. Dredge each tofu rectangle in wheat germ mixture.

4. Place rectangles in a single layer on the baking sheet. Bake until golden brown.

5. Let cool and serve with ketchup. Store leftovers in the fridge for up to 2 days.

egg salad

Eggs are packed with high-quality protein, so they are a great food for little ones. Grating the onion and celery gives this salad a boost of flavor without adding too much texture. Smear it on toasted bread or crackers.

PREP	5 to 10 minutes
YIELD	1 $\frac{1}{2}$ cups
SERVING SIZE	$\frac{1}{4}$ cup

3 hard-boiled eggs, peeled and rinsed

$\frac{1}{4}$ medium onion, peeled and grated

$\frac{1}{2}$ rib celery, grated

1 TB. mayonnaise

1 tsp. yellow mustard

1 TB. dill pickle relish or diced dill pickles

1. In a medium bowl, mash eggs with a large fork.

2. Add onion, celery, mayonnaise, mustard, and pickle relish and mix until well combined.

3. Serve immediately. Store leftovers in the fridge for up to 3 days.

note

You can substitute Greek yogurt for the mayonnaise if your kiddo does not have a problem with dairy. This will lend a little more protein and a tangy taste.

9 to 11 months

cooking *dried beans*

Black beans, pinto beans, and chickpeas can be used in lots of kid-friendly recipes, and they're a great source of healthy fiber and protein. Cooking your own beans from dried is economical and the results are tastier than using canned.

black *beans*

These cumin-scented beans make a great filling for enchiladas, quesadillas, or tacos, or just serve them on their own.

1 lb. (450g) dried black beans	1 large red onion, peeled and quartered	2 TB. ground cumin
2½ quarts (2.5l) water	4 garlic cloves, peeled and smashed	

PREP	10 minutes
COOK	1 to 2 hours
YIELD	6 cups
SERVING SIZE	2 tablespoons

1. In a colander, rinse beans and pick out any stones or bean hulls.

2. In a large heavy-bottomed saucepan, combine all ingredients. Bring to a boil and then reduce heat to low, partially cover, and simmer for an hour.

3. Check the beans. If they are not tender, continue simmering for an additional 30 to 60 minutes.

4. Transfer to a glass container on a cooling rack and cool for 15 to 20 minutes. Finish cooling in the fridge.

storing cooked beans

Cooked beans can be refrigerated in an airtight container for up to 1 week. Beans also freeze beautifully. For easy-to-use portions, place 1½ cups cooked beans into a quart-size zipper-lock freezer bag and freeze. These can be swapped in for recipes that call for a 15-oz. (425g) can of beans.

For black beans and pinto beans, store the beans with the cooking liquid. For chickpeas, drain first and then freeze.

pinto *beans*

Using the slow cooker makes this is a completely hands-off recipe. When cooked, you can serve pinto beans whole or mash them to make your own "refried" beans.

1 lb. (450g) dried pinto beans

2 quarts (2l) water

1 medium onion, peeled and quartered

2 cloves garlic, peeled and smashed

1 TB. ground cumin

1. In a colander, rinse beans and pick out any stones or bean hulls.

2. Place all ingredients in a medium slow cooker. Cover and cook on low for 8 to 10 hours.

3. Transfer to a glass container on a cooling rack and cool for 15 to 20 minutes. Then finish cooling in the fridge.

PREP	5 minutes
COOK	8 to 10 hours
YIELD	6 cups
SERVING SIZE	2 tablespoons
SPECIAL TOOLS	slow cooker

chickpeas *(garbanzo beans)*

More than any other bean, you can taste the difference between dried and canned chickpeas. Forget those slimy beans you are used to; chickpeas from dried are smooth, creamy, and packed with flavor.

3 cups dried chickpeas

1 TB. salt

1. Place the beans in a large, heavy-bottomed saucepan (like a Dutch oven). Cover with 2 inches (5cm) cold water. Bring to a boil over medium-high heat. Let simmer for 5 minutes.

2. Remove from heat. Let beans sit in warm water for 1 hour.

3. Drain and rinse beans in a colander with cold water. Place beans back in saucepan, add salt, and cover with 3 to 4 inches (7.5-10cm) cold water. Bring to a boil over medium-high heat and then cover and reduce heat to low. Simmer for 1 hour. Test for tenderness. The beans should be softened, but still firm. They continue to cook as they cool.

4. Let cool for 30 to 45 minutes and then continue cooling in the fridge.

PREP	5 minutes
COOK	2 to 3 hours
YIELD	6 cups
SERVING SIZE	2 tablespoons

slow-cooker baked beans

PREP	15 minutes
COOK	4 to 8 hours
YIELD	1 quart (1l)
SERVING SIZE	½ cup
SPECIAL TOOLS	slow cooker

These baked beans are a great addition to a barbecue or as a quick lunch. Beans are packed with fiber and protein. By making your own, you can reduce the amount of sugar and add a few veggies to the mix.

note

You can substitute great northern beans or navy beans for the pinto beans in this recipe.

2 (15-oz.; 425g) cans low-sodium pinto beans, rinsed and drained

1 medium white or yellow onion, finely chopped

1 sweet red, yellow, or orange pepper, finely chopped

1 tsp. garlic, minced

2 cups ketchup

2 TB. molasses

2 tsp. ground mustard

2 bay leaves

½ tsp. ground black pepper

1. Combine all ingredients in a medium slow cooker. Cook on low for 4 to 8 hours. The beans will be ready after 4 hours, but if you need to leave them in longer, the flavors will continue to meld.

2. Store leftovers in the fridge for up to 5 days or in the freezer for up to 3 months.

asian ground pork

This is one of our favorite, go-to weeknight dinners. It comes together quickly and makes great leftovers. Sweet and salty hoisin goes well with the mild taste of ground pork. You can easily slip in carrots and mushrooms to give this dish a nutritional punch with vitamin A and vitamin D. For some added crunch and texture, add chopped water chestnuts and bamboo shoots.

PREP	10 minutes
COOK	15 minutes
YIELD	5 to 6 cups
SERVING SIZE	½ cup

1 TB. grapeseed or canola oil OR ½ TB. grapeseed or canola oil and 2 tsp. sesame oil

1 bunch green onions, green and white ends, thinly sliced

1 cup sliced white mushrooms, finely chopped

½ cup shredded carrots, finely chopped

½ tsp. garlic, minced

2 tsp. fresh (or frozen) ginger, grated

1 lb. (450g) ground pork

1 (8-oz.; 225g) can water chestnuts, finely chopped, *optional*

1 (8-oz.; 225g) can bamboo shoots, finely chopped, *optional*

⅔ cup hoisin sauce

⅓ cup water

1 TB. seasoned rice vinegar

2 TB. fresh lime juice

1. In a large frying pan, heat oil over medium-high heat until shimmering. Add green onions, mushrooms, and carrots. Cook for 3 minutes until softened. Add garlic and ginger and cook for 30 seconds, until fragrant. Add pork and use a wooden spoon to break it up. Cook until pork is no longer pink, approximately 5 minutes. Drain fat.

2. Add water chestnuts and bamboo shoots, if using. Add hoisin sauce and water. Stir to combine. Add rice vinegar and lime juice. Simmer for 5 minutes. The sauce will thicken.

3. For adults, serve in butter lettuce cups with Sriracha sauce. For kiddos, serve alone or with Coconut Rice. Refrigerate leftovers in an airtight container for up to 3 days.

tip
This recipe requires a very large frying pan, especially if you add the water chestnuts and bamboo shoots. For high-volume recipes like this one, you may want to consider an electric skillet. I use mine way more than I care to admit—I even own two. I have pulled them both out on several occasions.

9 to 11 months

roasted salmon

This is my favorite method for cooking salmon. The lemon juice and flavor of the onions permeates the salmon and you get juicy, tangy onions as a bonus for the adults. You can change up the seasonings—try a smear of barbecue sauce or a dash of chili powder. Because salmon is so rich and cuts are so big, our family of three often shares one 8-ounce (170g) piece.

PREP	5 minutes
COOK	15 to 20 minutes
YIELD	1 filet
SERVING SIZE	2 tablespoons

1 small onion, sliced

1 small lemon, sliced

1 (6 to 8 oz.; 170 to 225g) salmon filet, deboned

1 TB. olive oil

¼ tsp. paprika

¼ tsp. ground black pepper

1. Preheat oven to 450°F (230°C). Line a rimmed baking sheet with foil.

2. Spread the onion slices on pan. Place the lemon slices over the onions and then place the salmon skin side down on top of the lemons and onions. Drizzle on olive oil and sprinkle with paprika and black pepper.

3. Roast for 15 to 20 minutes until salmon is opaque and flakes easily. If using a skin-on filet, remove the skin before serving. Store leftovers in the fridge for 1 day.

lemon dill sauce

It's fun for kiddos to dip just about anything, and salmon is no exception. To make a lemon dill dipping sauce to serve with the salmon, whisk together ¼ cup mayonnaise, the juice of 1 lemon, and ¼ tsp. dried dill.

italian meatballs

PREP	20 minutes
COOK	10 minutes
YIELD	50 meatballs
SERVING SIZE	2 meatballs

Meatballs are great for little hands and little mouths. The pork has a mild flavor, but you could substitute ground beef if you prefer. These meatballs come together in 30 minutes from start to finish. Using a cookie scoop makes portioning meatballs fast and easy; if you don't have one, it's a great investment. It will save you messy hands and lots of time.

½ medium onion, peeled and quartered

½ cup shredded carrot

½ cup sliced mushrooms

¼ cup roasted red peppers

1 lb. (450g) ground pork

1 egg

2 tsp. Italian seasoning

variations

To make **Egg-Free Italian Meatballs,** substitute ¼ cup marinara sauce for the egg. To make **Egg-Free Barbecue Turkey Meatballs,** replace carrot, mushrooms, and roasted red peppers with ½ cup frozen spinach (thawed) and ½ medium sweet pepper (chopped). Replace ground pork with 1 lb. (450g) ground turkey. Replace egg with ¼ cup barbecue sauce. Season with salt and pepper instead of Italian seasoning, and follow the same cooking instructions.

1. Line a large baking sheet with aluminum foil. Adjust oven racks so one is in the top position and the other is in the middle position. Preheat the broiler to high.

2. In a food processor fitted with a chopping blade, place onion, carrots, and mushrooms. Pulse until chopped. Add roasted red pepper. Pulse until all veggies are finely chopped but not puréed.

3. In a large bowl, combine veggie mixture with ground pork, egg, and Italian seasoning. Use your hands to mix together.

4. Using a cookie scoop, scoop half-tablespoon portions of the meat mixture and place on the pan. Do not reshape with your hands. Depending on the size of the pan, you may need two pans.

5. Place the pan on the top rack and broil for 5 minutes. Move pan to the middle rack and broil for an additional 3 to 4 minutes, until meatballs are browned and cooked through.

6. Spread a sheet of aluminum foil on the counter and transfer meatballs to the foil. This will keep the fat from sticking to the meatballs.

7. Leftovers can be kept in the fridge for up to 5 days or in the freezer for up to 3 months. To reheat from frozen, place frozen meatballs on a tray in a 400°F (200°C) oven. Bake 15 to 20 minutes until heated through.

9 to 11 months

chicken noodle *soup*

Before having kids, I had a very different chicken noodle soup recipe that called for homemade stock and simmering for hours. This soup tastes just as good, has very little required chopping, and can be made in less than 40 minutes. Chicken breast tenders cook quickly in the broth, giving it great flavor and requiring little prep work. Add the noodles when serving (or leave them out), as they are quick to get mushy and don't freeze well.

PREP	5 minutes
COOK	30 minutes
YIELD	3 quarts (3l)
SERVING SIZE	½ cup

1 medium onion, diced

3 ribs celery, diced

1 TB. olive or grapeseed oil

2 qt. (2l) high-quality chicken broth

2 tsp. Better Than Bouillon Chicken Base

2 bay leaves

¼ tsp. dried parsley

¼ tsp. dried sage

¼ tsp. dried rosemary

¼ tsp. dried thyme

1 lb. (450g) chicken breast tenders

1 (10-oz.; 285g) bag frozen mixed vegetables

3 TB. to ½ cup dried noodles, depending on the serving size

1. In a large, heavy-bottomed pot, heat oil over high heat until shimmering. Add onions and celery and sauté for 5 minutes or until soft.

2. While onion and celery are cooking, cut chicken tenders into bite-size pieces. Once onion and celery are softened, add parsley, sage, rosemary, and thyme. Sauté for 1 minute.

3. Add broth, Better Than Bouillon, and bay leaves. Bring to a boil. Add chicken. Return to a boil. Reduce heat to medium and simmer for 2 minutes.

4. Add vegetables and cook for an additional 6 minutes. Separate the portion that you will be eating immediately. Add noodles to that portion and simmer for 4 to 7 minutes until pasta is tender.

5. Refrigerate in an airtight container for up to 5 days or store in the freezer for up to 3 months.

9 to 11 months

frozen fruit pops

PREP	15 minutes
FREEZE	3 to 4 hours
YIELD	1½ cups or 6 (2-oz.; 50ml) fruit pops
SERVING SIZE	1 fruit pop
SPECIAL TOOLS	ice pop mold

Frozen fruit pops are the solution to two major problems: they help with teething, and they keep your kiddo occupied while you finish dinner—all while providing nutritious fruit. I make my frozen fruit pops as thick as possible because I want it to be mostly fruit. A little liquid makes blending easier, and if your child can tolerate dairy, you can add ½ cup yogurt for a boost of protein and calcium.

½ cup frozen peaches, partially thawed

½ cup frozen blueberries, partially thawed

½ whole frozen banana

¼ to ½ cup liquid of your choice (unsweetened apple juice, milk, or water)

1. Place all ingredients in a blender and purée until smooth.

2. Scoop into ice pop molds. Freeze for 3 to 4 hours.

3. Store in freezer for up to 1 month.

note

Any leftover purée can be eaten like a sorbet. The banana makes it creamy, so share it with your kiddo as a special treat.

selecting fruits

You can customize these pops to your tastes and what you have on hand. To get the best combinations, keep these things in mind:

A **frozen banana** or **frozen mango** will add sweetness and creaminess to your pop.

I always include **blueberries** in my frozen pops. They are sweet and colorful, and pack a lot of vitamin C.

Peaches can be handy when dealing with constipation issues. They add tartness, so you will need to balance it with a sweeter fruit.

Balance **sweet fruits** (bananas, strawberries, raspberries, blueberries, cherries, pears, dates, prunes) with **tart fruits** (peaches, blackberries, mango, pineapple).

9 to 11 months

variation

To make **Fruit and Yogurt Ice Pops**, replace liquid with ½ cup plain whole-milk yogurt. For a dairy-free version, try full-fat coconut milk instead of yogurt.

baby biscotti

PREP	20 minutes
COOK	65 to 70 minutes
YIELD	30 bars
SERVING SIZE	1 bar

Biscotti are a natural teething treat for your kiddo and also a great snack for you with your morning coffee. They may take a long time to bake, but they are easy to make and store well. To make the raisins nice and plump, soak them in warm water while you assemble the other ingredients.

½ cup raisins

2 cups whole-wheat pastry flour

1 tsp. baking powder

⅛ tsp. salt

1 tsp. ground cinnamon

¼ tsp. ground nutmeg

¼ cup unsalted butter, softened

¼ cup unsweetened applesauce

⅓ cup sugar

2 eggs

1 tsp. vanilla

1. Preheat oven to 350°F (180°C). Line a baking sheet with parchment paper. Place the raisins in a small bowl of warm water to soak.

2. In a medium bowl, whisk together whole-wheat pastry flour, baking powder, salt, cinnamon, and nutmeg.

3. In a large bowl, beat butter, applesauce, and sugar until butter is evenly distributed. Add eggs and vanilla. Stir to combine.

4. Pour dry ingredients into the wet ingredients and stir until combined. Drain water from raisins and fold them into the batter.

5. Divide dough into four equal sections. Shape into loaves, approximately 4 inches (10cm) wide and 1 inch (2.5cm) high. The dough will be sticky!

6. Bake 20 to 25 minutes until edges are golden brown. Remove from oven and place on a cooling rack. Let dough cool on pan for 10 minutes. During that time, reduce the oven temperature to 325°F (170°C).

7. Cut dough into ½-inch (1cm) slices. Place slices on the baking sheet cut side down and bake for an additional 25 minutes. Let cool on pan.

8. Store leftovers at room temperature for up to 5 days or in the freezer for up to 3 months. For extra-crisp biscotti, do not cover for 12 to 24 hours.

coconut rice

I love playing with rice recipes, and after lots of experimenting, I found a great combination of sweet, savory, and tangy. The coconut milk is a perfect partner to brown basmati rice, and the lime adds a little zing. Don't be afraid of the brown bits on the bottom of the pan. Stir them into the creamy rice for texture and taste. For adults, pair this with spicy meats and protein. For kids, try the mango variation.

PREP	10 minutes
COOK	40 minutes
YIELD	3 cups
SERVING SIZE	1/4 cup

1 cup brown basmati or jasmine rice

1 (13.6-oz.; 403ml) can full-fat coconut milk, shaken

1 cup water

Juice of 1 large lime, approximately 1/4 cup

1/2 TB. honey or sugar

1/2 tsp. salt

1. Rinse rice until water runs clear.

2. In a large saucepan, combine rice, coconut milk, lime juice, honey, water, and salt.

3. Bring to a boil over medium-high heat. Stir, reduce heat to low, and cover.

4. Simmer 30 to 40 minutes. Stir occasionally.

5. Serve immediately. Store leftovers in the fridge for up to 5 days.

variations

For **Mango Coconut Rice**, stir in 2 cups diced mango.

For **Spanish Rice**, replace cup of water with 2 1/2 cups water, and replace coconut milk with 1 (15.5-oz.; 440g) jar salsa (approximately 1 1/2 cups). Omit lime juice, salt, and honey. Follow the same cooking instructions. Serve with shredded cheddar cheese and black beans.

part 5

12 to 17 months

Congratulations! You made it to the 1-year mark. Your little one is now entering the new phase of toddlerhood. With this stage comes many changes. The first common change is weaning from bottle or breast. Second, most kiddos make the big transition to "table food" at this point, which just means eating many of the same foods as you. In this section, you'll find lots of recipes that will please toddlers and grown-ups alike!

what baby is eating now: *table foods*

Now that your kiddo is getting better at finger feeding and chewing, it's time to graduate to table food. This means she can eat the same foods as the rest of the family, as long as it's chopped into pieces she can handle.

At this stage, most babies can completely self-feed by picking up food with their fingers. They also may be interested in practicing with a spoon, but be prepared for messes!

Cow's Milk

Once your child turns 1, you can start to wean from breast or bottle and offer whole milk in a cup. If you are breastfeeding and want to continue, you can do so for as long as you feel it's right for you and your child.

Cow's milk is low in iron, and drinking a lot of it can interfere with your child's ability to absorb iron. Too much milk can also fill up your child and make her less likely to eat from other food groups. Keep milk intake to 2 cups per day (16 oz.; 470ml). Children should drink whole milk until age 2.

Choking Prevention

Your little one is no longer on baby food, so there are a few things to keep in mind:

- Avoid smooth, round pieces like whole grapes, hot dog rounds, raw baby carrots, pickles, and whole nuts. Cut these foods into smaller pieces to make them safe for your child.

- In general, cutting food into strips is safer than chunks. Of course, chunks of really soft food are just fine.

- Tender cooked meats and ground meats are easiest for toddlers to chew. Steak or chicken breast should be finely chopped.

- It's still a good idea to peel the skin off of most fruits and vegetables.

- Don't let your child walk around or run while eating.

Other Changes

- Your child can now safely consume honey. Just like other sugars in your child's diet, honey should be given in small amounts.

- After age 1, it's normal for your child to become more picky. Keep providing a variety of foods and textures for her to try.

- You may see a lull in your child's appetite. Kids at this stage become very active and less interested in food. Providing two healthy snacks per day can help your child get additional nutrition between meals. If you are weaning, these snacks can be given at the times your baby received breast milk or formula.

nutritional needs: 12 to 17 *months*

After 12 months, your child's growth will begin to slow. Each month, you can expect an additional 7 to 11 ounces (200–275g) for weight, and 0.3 inch (1cm) for height. The most important thing is that your child grows at a steady rate, no matter what shape or size she is.

It's also common for kids at this stage to be restless during meals. Try your best. Remember, you can only provide the food; you can't make your child eat it. Here are approximate serving sizes for a child at this stage.

Food Group	Servings per Day	One Serving Equals
Grains	6	¼ slice bread; ¼ cup cereal, rice, or pasta; 1 to 2 crackers
Vegetables	2 to 3	1 TB. cooked or raw veggies
Fruits	2	1 TB. cooked or ¼ cup raw fruit
Dairy	2	4 oz. (100ml) milk, 1-inch (2.5cm) cube of cheese, 4 oz. (110g) yogurt
Protein	2	2 TB. ground meat or flaked fish, 1 egg, 2 TB. beans, 2 TB. nut butter

Nutritional Spotlight: Calcium

Calcium is an important mineral at this stage of development. Between the ages of 1 and 3, kids need more than three times the amount needed from birth to age 1.

Calcium is used to build strong bones, and it helps muscles and nerves work properly. Getting enough calcium early on will help prevent your child from having bone-related diseases later in life.

Dairy products are rich in calcium, and it can also be found in many plant foods.

RECIPE TO TRY: Mac 'n' Greens

foods rich in calcium

Yogurt

Cow's milk

Cheese

Plant milk

Collard greens

Kale

Broccoli

Almond butter

Beans

meal plans:
12 to 17 months

Here are daily and weekly meal plans for feeding your toddler at this stage. Please note that every child is different. This is only meant to be a guide, not a strict schedule.

Sample Feeding Schedule

TIME	SLEEP AND FOOD
6:00–7:00 AM	Wake up for the day.
7:15–7:30 AM	Breakfast: protein (yogurt, egg) + fruit **or** whole grain + fruit
9:00 AM	Nap for 1 hour.
10:00 AM	Snack: fruit or vegetable + milk **or** whole grain + milk
12:00 PM	Lunch: protein + veggie + starch
1:00 PM	Nap for 1 to 2 hours.
3:00 PM	Snack: fruit or vegetable + milk **or** whole grain + milk
5:00–6:00 PM	Dinner: protein + veggie + starch
7:00–7:30 PM	Nurse or provide milk before bed, at your discretion.

Meal Key

Protein = meat, beans, lentils, eggs, fish, yogurt, cheese

Starch = whole grains, potatoes, peas, winter squash (butternut, acorn), and corn

Veggie = any veggie other than potatoes, peas, winter squash, or corn

Sample Weekly Meal Plan

DAY	MEALS
Monday	**Breakfast:** 1 scrambled egg + 1 TB. chopped avocado **Snack:** ¼ cup applesauce + 4 oz. (100ml) whole milk **Lunch:** 1 Cheese and Veggie Quesadilla **Snack:** 2 Wheat Crackers spread with Almond Butter + 4 oz. (100ml) whole milk **Dinner:** small slice of Veggie Meatloaf, chopped + 3 Crispy Baked Potato Fries, cut up
Tuesday	**Breakfast:** 4 oz. (110g) Homemade Yogurt + 1 kiwi, chopped **Snack:** 3 cucumber slices with Hummus + 4 oz. (100ml) milk **Lunch:** small slice of LO Veggie Meatloaf, chopped + 3 Crispy Baked Potato Fries, cut up **Snack:** ¼ cup applesauce + 4 oz. (100ml) milk **Dinner:** 2 TB. Barbecue Chicken + ¼ cup Mac 'n' Greens
Wednesday	**Breakfast:** ¼ cup oatmeal and 2-4 TB. banana, chopped **Snack:** 1 chopped kiwi + 4 oz. (100ml) milk **Lunch:** 2 TB. LO Barbecue Chicken + ¼ cup LO Mac 'n' Greens **Snack:** 2 Wheat Crackers with Almond Butter + 4 oz. (100ml) milk **Dinner:** ¼ cup pasta with Spaghetti Sauce + 2 TB. steamed broccoli
Thursday	**Breakfast:** 1 scrambled egg + 1 TB. chopped avocado **Snack:** ¼ cup applesauce + 4 oz. (100ml) milk **Lunch:** ¼ cup LO pasta with Spaghetti Sauce + 2 TB. LO steamed broccoli **Snack:** 3 cucumber slices dipped in Hummus + 4 oz. (100ml) milk **Dinner:** 2-4 TB. Sweet Potato and Greens Soup + ½ Grilled Cheese Sandwich (made with one piece of bread) cut into pieces
Friday	**Breakfast:** 4 oz. (110g) Homemade Yogurt + 1 chopped kiwi **Snack:** 2 Wheat Crackers spread with Almond Butter + 4 oz. (100ml) milk **Lunch:** 2-4 TB. LO Sweet Potato and Greens Soup + ¼ Grilled Cheese Sandwich **Snack:** 2-4 TB. chopped banana + 4 oz. (100ml) milk **Dinner:** 2 TB. Mexican Chicken + 1 TB. black beans + 1 TB. avocado
Saturday	**Breakfast:** French Toast Bites (½ slice of bread) + 2-4 TB. chopped banana **Snack:** ¼ cup grapes, halved + 4 oz. (100ml) milk **Lunch:** quesadilla made with LO Mexican Chicken and veggies **Snack:** 3 thin bell pepper strips dipped in Hummus + 4 oz. (100ml) milk **Dinner:** ¼-½ cup Baby Chili + 1 small slice Cheddar Apple Bread, cut up
Sunday	**Breakfast:** ½ cup Baked Oatmeal **Snack:** small slice Cheddar Apple Bread + 4 oz. (100ml) milk **Lunch:** ¼-½ cup LO Baby Chili + 1 TB. avocado **Snack:** ¼ cup grapes, halved + 4 oz. (100ml) milk **Dinner:** 2 TB. Roasted Salmon + ¼ cup rice + 1 TB. sautéed zucchini rounds

french toast *bites*

PREP	5 minutes
COOK	20 minutes
YIELD	6 to 8 slices
SERVING SIZE	½ slice

Yes, French toast is a treat in the morning, but let's take a closer look: whole-grain bread, eggs, and milk. By adding cinnamon and vanilla to the mix, you need less maple syrup. I would go as far to say that this is a healthy breakfast dish. Wouldn't you?

3 large eggs

¼ cup milk or non-dairy milk

¼ tsp. ground cinnamon

1 tsp. vanilla extract

⅓ to ½ cup maple syrup (optional)

1 to 2 TB. butter

6 to 8 slices of bread

1. In a shallow bowl, whisk eggs, milk, cinnamon, vanilla, and maple syrup, if using.

2. In a large frying pan or griddle, melt butter over medium heat. Dip a slice of bread in the egg mixture, covering both sides, and place in frying pan. Repeat with remaining slices of bread. Cook 6 to 8 minutes on each side, until golden brown.

3. Cut into bite-size pieces and serve immediately. For any leftovers, cool to room temperature, and store in a zipper-lock freezer bag. Bites will be good for up to 1 month. To thaw, place in fridge the night before or let sit at room temperature for 30 minutes to an hour.

tip

Adding maple syrup to the batter means you don't have to worry about sticky fingers and sticky faces after breakfast. Start with ⅓ cup. Remember that little ones are super tasters, so though it may not seem sweet to you, it may be sweet enough for them.

12 to 17 months

baked oatmeal

This is a cozy and nutritious breakfast for cold mornings. Prep it the night before and then pop it in the oven in the morning. It's great reheated, so you can also make it on the weekend and eat it throughout the week. Your little one will love the natural sweetness from the fruits and the array of textures. You'll love how easy it is to make a warm, complete breakfast.

PREP	15 minutes
COOK	50 minutes to 1 hour
YIELD	6 cups
SERVING SIZE	1/4 cup

2 bananas, sliced

1 apple, diced

1/2 cup berries, fresh or frozen

2 cups rolled or old-fashioned oats

1 tsp. baking powder

2 tsp. ground cinnamon

1/2 tsp. ground nutmeg

1/2 tsp. salt

1 large egg

2 cups milk or non-dairy milk

1/4 cup maple syrup

2 TB. butter, cold and cut into small chunks

1. Grease an 8×8-inch (20×20cm) cake pan with cooking spray. Preheat the oven to 350°F (180°C).

2. Spread the banana, apple, and berries in the greased pan.

3. In a medium bowl, mix together the rolled oats, baking powder, cinnamon, nutmeg, and salt. Pour oat mixture over the fruit in the pan.

4. In the same bowl, whisk together the egg, milk, and maple syrup. Pour milk mixture over oats. Scatter chunks of butter on top.

5. Bake for 50 minutes to 1 hour until the top is golden brown. Store any leftovers in the fridge for up to 1 week.

notes

To prep the night before, follow steps 1 through 4 and store in the fridge overnight. Bake the next morning.

To make dairy-free, substitute your favorite non-dairy milk for the milk and replace the butter with coconut oil.

12 to 17 months

whole-grain waffles

Nothing makes a morning special faster than a home-made waffle. And the beauty of this recipe, in addition to being dairy free and whole grain, is that you can make your own stash of freezer waffles, so even weekday mornings can have that special Saturday feel.

PREP	5 minutes
COOK	15 to 20 minutes
YIELD	5 large waffles
SERVING SIZE	¼ waffle
SPECIAL TOOLS	waffle iron

2 cups whole-wheat pastry flour

2 TB. sugar

½ tsp. cinnamon

¼ tsp. ground nutmeg

2 tsp. baking powder

½ tsp. salt

2 eggs

1 tsp. vanilla extract

1½ cups carbonated water

¼ cup mild-tasting oil (canola or grapeseed)

1. Turn on waffle iron to preheat. Preheat oven to 200°F (90°C).

2. In a large bowl, whisk together whole-wheat pastry flour, sugar, cinnamon, nutmeg, baking powder, and salt.

3. In a medium bowl, whisk together eggs. Add vanilla, carbonated water, and oil. Whisk together. Pour into dry ingredients and stir just until combined.

4. Grease the waffle iron with an oil spray. Cook waffles according to manufacturer's instructions. Keep waffles in oven until ready to serve.

5. Store leftovers in the fridge for up to 5 days or freeze for up to 3 months. Waffles can be reheated from frozen in a toaster.

tip

The easiest way to freeze waffles is to place them in a zipper-lock bag separated by wax paper. Label the bag with the type of waffles and the date.

12 to 17 months

variations

You can make variations by the single waffle or by the whole batch. I prefer doing variations by waffle so you can enjoy a wider variety of flavors.

For **Cinnamon Sugar Waffles**, mix ½ TB. sugar with ½ TB. cinnamon. Pour the batter into waffle iron and dust with cinnamon sugar. To make a whole batch, mix 2½ TB. sugar and 2½ TB. cinnamon with the batter.

For **Blueberry Waffles**, sprinkle 3 TB. fresh blueberries on top of the batter in the waffle iron, or mix a cup of fresh blueberries into the batter. You can also use chopped fresh strawberries to make **Strawberry Waffles**. Do not use frozen fruit.

For **Chocolate Chip Waffles**, sprinkle 2 TB. mini chocolate chips on the batter in the waffle iron, or stir ¾ cup mini chocolate chips into the batter.

whole—grain pumpkin muffins

PREP	20 minutes
COOK	20 to 25 minutes
YIELD	12 muffins
SERVING SIZE	1 muffin

Made with yogurt and applesauce, this is a muffin you can feel good about giving your kiddo. The raisins add a little burst of sweetness, and the pumpkin is loaded with vitamin C and beta-carotene.

2 cups whole-wheat pastry flour

2 tsp. baking powder

½ tsp. baking soda

1 TB. pumpkin pie spice

½ tsp. salt

1 (15.5-oz.; 440g) can pumpkin purée

⅓ cup unsweetened applesauce

½ cup plain yogurt

½ cup brown sugar, packed

¼ cup sugar

2 large eggs

1 tsp. vanilla extract

⅔ cup raisins

1. Preheat oven to 375°F (190°C). Grease a 12-cup muffin pan.

2. In a large bowl, whisk together whole-wheat pastry flour, baking powder, baking soda, pumpkin pie spice, and salt.

3. In a medium bowl, whisk together eggs and then add pumpkin purée, applesauce, plain yogurt, brown sugar, sugar, and vanilla extract. Stir until combined.

4. Pour wet ingredients into dry ingredients. Stir until just incorporated. Gently fold in the raisins.

5. Pour in the prepared muffin pan and bake for 20 to 25 minutes until a toothpick inserted in a muffin comes out clean.

6. Cool in the pan for 5 minutes and then remove muffins from pan and cool on a cooling rack. Store muffins in an airtight container in the fridge for up to 1 week or in the freezer for up to 3 months.

smoothies

Smoothies are endlessly adaptable and a great way to slip some extra veggies or protein into a sweet treat. Experiment with your own variations using your little one's favorite ingredients. If you have leftovers, pour them into an ice pop mold for another icy treat.

cherry berry *smoothie*

½ cup dark sweet frozen cherries	½ cup frozen peaches	½ tsp. ground flaxseed
½ cup frozen blueberries	2 TB. silken tofu	1 cup milk or nondairy milk
	Generous handful raw spinach	

PREP	10 minutes
YIELD	2 cups
SERVING SIZE	½ cup

1. In a blender, combine cherries, blueberries, peaches, tofu, spinach, ground flaxseed, and milk. Purée until smooth.

2. Serve immediately.

chocolate peanut butter *smoothie*

1 cup frozen blueberries	1 TB. peanut butter	½ tsp. ground flaxseed
1 frozen banana	3 TB. cocoa powder	1 cup milk or nondairy milk
Small handful raw spinach	2 dates, pitted	

PREP	10 minutes
YIELD	2 cups
SERVING SIZE	½ cup

1. Place dates in a small bowl and cover with hot water. Let dates sit for 5 minutes to soften and then drain.

2. In a blender, combine blueberries, banana, spinach, peanut butter, cocoa powder, dates, ground flaxseed, and milk. Purée until smooth.

3. Serve immediately.

tip
If nut allergies are a concern, omit the peanut butter for an equally delicious chocolate berry smoothie.

12 to 17 months

quesadillas

PREP	5 minutes
COOK	5 minutes
YIELD	1 quesadilla
SERVING SIZE	½ quesa-dilla

Quesadillas are my gateway food. When I want my daughter to eat something, I put it in a quesadilla. Leftovers? Make a quesadilla. Veggies? Make a quesadilla. It's quick, it's hot, and it's an easy sell to a kiddo. Experiment with different ingredient combinations using this basic formula.

1 10-inch (25cm) whole-wheat tortilla

2 TB. filling of your choice

2 TB. shredded cheese

½ TB. salsa or sauce of your choice

1. In a small bowl, combine filling, cheese, and sauce. Spread on half of a whole-wheat tortilla.

2. Heat a medium skillet over medium-high heat.

3. Place filled tortilla in dry pan and heat for 2 minutes. Flip over tortilla, and heat for 1 more minute. Flip over again, and heat for 30 seconds to 1 minute more, until tortilla is golden brown on both sides and cheese is melted.

4. Cut into squares with a pizza cutter. Serve when it's cooled enough for your kiddo.

nutritional note

Try to select 100 percent whole-grain tortillas. You'll know it's whole grain if the first ingredient is "whole-grain wheat flour." If the words "enriched flour" appear, it is not whole grain.

quesadilla combos to try

Quesadillas are a great way to refashion leftovers. You can make the filling using just about any cooked meat, bean, or veggie mixed with cheese and sauce. Try these combos:

Salmon + Swiss cheese + barbecue sauce

Hamburger + ketchup + cheddar cheese

Pork + diced apple + cheddar cheese

Chicken + barbecue sauce + cheddar cheese

Mashed meatball + marinara sauce + mozzarella cheese

Broccoli + cheddar cheese

variations

For a **Classic Quesadilla,** omit the salsa and filling and use 3 TB. shredded cheese. For a **Salsa Quesadilla,** omit the added filling.

ham and cheese *pocket*

PREP	5 minutes
COOK	5 minutes
YIELD	1 pocket
SERVING SIZE	½ pocket

Similar to a quesadilla, this little lunch number is an easy win for kiddos. Less work than a grilled cheese, it's a nice way to sneak some meat into your toddler's diet. Try swapping the deli ham for nitrate-free turkey, chicken, or roast beef deli meat.

1 10-inch (25cm) whole-wheat tortilla

1 piece nitrate-free deli ham

2 TB. shredded cheese

1. Sprinkle a tablespoon of cheese over half of the whole-wheat tortilla. Place ham on top of cheese. Top with remaining cheese. Fold tortilla over to cover the filling.

2. Heat a medium skillet over medium-high heat. Place filled tortilla in dry pan. Heat for 2 minutes, then flip. Heat for 1 more minute. Flip. Heat for an additional 30 seconds to 1 minute until tortilla is golden brown on both sides and cheese is melted.

3. Cut into squares with a pizza cutter. Serve when it's cooled enough for your kiddo.

grilled cheese *sandwich*

Grilled cheese sandwiches are a special treat in our household. My version has an extra-crispy crust, an ooey-gooey cheese filling, and a punch of protein and fiber from hummus. I serve it cut into bite-size pieces with some ketchup and a side of veggies and hummus.

PREP	5 minutes
COOK	3 to 5 minutes
YIELD	1 sandwich
SERVING SIZE	½ sandwich

2 slices whole-wheat bread

1 TB. hummus

½ TB. unsalted butter, softened

3 to 4 TB. shredded cheddar cheese

1. Spread butter on one side of both slices of bread. Spread hummus on the unbuttered side of one slice.

2. Spray a medium skillet with cooking spray and heat over medium-high heat.

3. Place the slice of bread with hummus in the pan, buttered side down. Sprinkle cheese over hummus and then top with the other slice of bread, buttered side facing up.

4. Cook on one side for 2 to 3 minutes. Flip sandwich and cook 1 more minute. Serve immediately.

toasting your grilled cheese

Grilled cheese sandwiches are a lot like toasted marshmallows. There are some, like me, who like them with a little black on the outside. And there are others with the patience to rotate often to get that perfectly golden toasted cheese.

If you don't like any black on your grilled cheese, flip every minute and keep a close eye. It may take a little longer, but you will get a perfectly toasted cheese sandwich.

variations

To make **Peanut Butter**, use 2 cups peanuts and omit the almonds and sunflower seeds. To make **Almond Butter**, use 2 cups almonds and omit the sunflower seeds and peanuts.

nut and seed *butter*

Nut and seed butters are so easy to make, and kiddos love seeing how their favorite spreads are made. Almonds have a lot of health benefits, but straight-up almond or sunflower seed butter can be a little too rich. This mix of nuts and seeds provides the bonus nutrition with a mild taste.

PREP	10 minutes
YIELD	2 cups
SERVING SIZE	1 tablespoon
SPECIAL TOOLS	food processor

½ cup roasted, unsalted peanuts

½ cup raw sunflower seeds

1 cup dry roasted almonds

¼ cup mild oil (canola or grapeseed)

1. In a food processor fitted with a chopping blade, combine peanuts, sunflower seeds, and almonds. Process for 1 minute until the nuts and seeds are chopped and mixed.

2. Continue processing and slowly pour in the oil, stopping to scrape down the sides of the bowl with a spatula when necessary.

3. Transfer to an airtight container and store at room temperature for up to 2 weeks. Store in the fridge for up to 1 month.

nutritional note

Nuts and seeds are rich in healthy fats that are important for your child's heart, brain, and nervous system. Other key nutrients in nuts and seeds include vitamin E, magnesium, potassium, and fiber. By making your own nut butter, you avoid the partially hydrogenated oils (trans fats) and added sugars found in many store-bought varieties.

roasting almonds

It's easy to roast your own almonds for nut butter. Simply place a single layer of raw almonds on a rimmed baking sheet. Bake at 350°F (180°C) for 17 to 18 minutes. When you can smell the nuts, pull them out. They will continue roasting (and crisping) as they cool, so err on the side of under-done rather than overdone.

baby chili

PREP	10 minutes
COOK	25 minutes
YIELD	3 quarts (3l)
SERVING SIZE	½ cup

This hearty tomato-based soup features protein-rich ground beef and beans as well as a healthy dose of veggies. To make it suitable for young palates, the only spice element in this "chili" comes from the chiles in the diced tomatoes. If your kiddo can handle it, feel free to add a pinch of chili powder, but remember: kids are super tasters. A hint of spice for you is a mouthful of spice for them.

taking shortcuts

It's okay to take a few shortcuts once in a while. Pre-cooked ingredients like tomato soup and canned beans can make make life a little easier. Just avoid highly processed foods that include unwanted ingredients, like high-fructose corn syrup.

1 cup uncooked whole-wheat pasta (spirals or elbow macaroni)

1 TB. olive oil, canola oil, or grapeseed oil

1 large onion, diced

3 celery ribs, diced

2 medium carrots, peeled and diced

1 lb. (450g) grass-fed ground beef

¼ tsp. salt

¼ tsp ground black pepper

1 (15-oz.; 425g) can kidney beans, rinsed and drained

1½ cups frozen corn

2 qt. (2l) low-sodium tomato soup

1 (14.5-oz.; 411g) can diced tomatoes with chiles

1. Cook pasta according to package directions, but boil it 1 minute less than directed. Drain pasta in a colander and set aside.

2. In a large frying pan, heat oil over medium-high heat. Add onion, carrots, and celery. Cook until softened, approximately 3 minutes.

3. Add beef. Season with salt and pepper. Brown meat, breaking apart with a wooden spoon until no longer pink. Drain fat.

4. In a large saucepan, combine tomato soup, kidney beans, corn, cooked pasta, diced tomatoes, and meat mixture. Cook over medium-high heat until warmed through, approximately 10 minutes. Reduce heat and simmer until you are ready to serve.

5. Store leftovers in the fridge for up to 1 week or in the freezer for up to 3 months.

sweet potato and greens *soup*

PREP	15 minutes
COOK	50 minutes
YIELD	3 quarts (3l)
SERVING SIZE	½ cup
SPECIAL TOOLS	immersion blender

This soup is creamy, decadent, and packed with healthy super foods. The sweet potato adds sweetness and the garam masala is the perfect blend of warmth and spice. The warm spices highlight a new, comforting side of spinach and kale.

5 cups vegetable broth

3 medium sweet potatoes, diced

1 medium potato, diced

16 oz. (450g) fresh spinach

2 bunches kale, stems removed and roughly chopped

1½ TB. olive oil

2 medium onions, chopped

1 bunch green onions, white and green ends, chopped

1 bunch cilantro, stems removed and roughly chopped

1 to 2 cups water

2 to 3 TB. fresh lemon juice

1 TB. garam masala

½ tsp. salt

½ tsp. ground black pepper

1. In a large stockpot, combine 4 cups vegetable broth, sweet potatoes, potato, spinach, and kale. Bring to a boil. Reduce heat to low and simmer for 15 minutes.

2. Meanwhile, heat olive oil in a medium frying pan over medium-high heat. Add onions and sauté for 3 to 4 minutes. Once they start sizzling, reduce heat to low and stir occasionally to prevent burning. Sauté onions until the greens and potatoes are done simmering, about 20 to 30 minutes.

3. Add sautéed onions, green onions, and cilantro to potato and greens mixture. Add remaining 1 cup vegetable broth and 1 cup water. Simmer for 10 minutes.

4. Add lemon juice, garam masala, salt, and pepper. Remove from heat. Using an immersion blender, purée the soup. Add an additional 1 cup water if you would like a thinner soup. Taste and season as you purée. Serve immediately.

5. Store leftovers in an airtight container in the fridge for up to 1 week or in the freezer for up to 3 months.

tip

Though the soup won't fill a stockpot, the tall walls keep the soup from splattering when using the immersion blender.

If you don't have an immersion blender, you can purée the soup in a regular blender. Fill the blender only halfway, and cover loosely with a dish towel. Be very cautious.

12 to 17 months

crispy crunchy breadsticks

These breadsticks are not only delicious, but are also great for teething kiddos and a good way to use day-old bread. I have to credit Melissa D'Arabian for the idea, but I have tweaked her recipe to make it more kid-friendly. These breadsticks are great for dunking in soups or marinara sauce.

PREP	10 to 15 minutes
COOK	10 minutes
YIELD	16 breadsticks
SERVING SIZE	1 breadstick

½ whole-wheat baguette

¼ cup grapeseed oil

¼ tsp. garlic salt

1 tsp. dried basil

½ tsp. ground black pepper

1. Preheat oven to 400°F (200°C). Line a baking sheet with parchment paper.

2. In a small bowl, whisk together oil, garlic salt, basil, and ground black pepper.

3. Cut the heels off the baguette. Quarter the baguette by cutting in half horizontally and then vertically. Cut each quarter into 4 strips.

4. Brush each strip with the oil mixture and place on prepared sheet.

5. Bake for 10 minutes until outsides are crisp. Cool to room temperature and serve. Store in a zipper-lock bag for up to 1 day.

make it your own

You can use day-old bread to get a crisp breadstick. If you use fresh bread, the inside will be doughy. Both are delicious! You can also use any shape of bread (not just a baguette), as long as you cut it into uniform strips. Play with the seasonings to match your family's tastes. Try garlic powder and Parmesan cheese to make garlic breadsticks.

12 to 17 months

lime chickpea quinoa salad

This is a quick and refreshing salad for summertime. Little ones will enjoy practicing their pincer grasp with the creamy chickpeas. Quinoa provides a complete plant protein and chickpeas add both fiber and iron, while the lime juice helps your kiddo absorb that iron. Serve on its own or with baked tortilla chips for dipping.

PREP	20 minutes
YIELD	3 to 4 cups
SERVING SIZE	1/3 cup

1 1/2 cups cooked chickpeas, or 1 (15.5-oz.; 425g) can chickpeas, rinsed and drained

1 1/2 cups quinoa, cooked

Small handful cilantro, finely chopped (approximately 1/2 cup)

1/2 medium red bell pepper, finely diced

1 clove garlic, minced

2 TB. olive oil

Juice of 2 or 3 limes, approximately 1/3 to 1/2 cup

1/4 to 1/2 tsp. ground cumin

1. In a medium bowl, whisk together oil, garlic, lime juice, and cumin.

2. Add chickpeas, quinoa, cilantro, and red bell pepper. Gently stir to combine.

3. Refrigerate leftovers in an airtight container for up to 5 days. The taste gets better with time as the lime juice and seasonings infuse the rest of the salad.

nutritional note

Did you know a red bell pepper has more vitamin C than an orange? Vitamin C keeps little ones healthy by boosting their immune systems, and helps their bodies build new tissue and bone. It can also help them absorb iron from their food.

preparing quinoa

Use a 2:1 ratio when cooking quinoa: 2 cups liquid for 1 cup dry quinoa. You can use water, but vegetable or chicken broth will add more flavor.

In a medium saucepan, combine liquid and quinoa. Bring to a boil over medium-high heat, then cover and reduce heat to low. Simmer for 10 minutes, fluff, and it's ready to go.

citrus beet salad

PREP	10 minutes
MARINATE	8 hours
YIELD	2 cups
SERVING SIZE	1/3 cup

Beets are an excellent source of potassium and fiber, but their earthy flavor can be overwhelming for little ones. In this recipe, the orange juice and apple cider vinegar mellow out the strong beet flavor. The longer it marinates, the sweeter and milder the beets will taste.

Juice of 1 orange (approximately 3 TB.)

2 tsp. Dijon mustard

1 TB. mild oil (grapeseed or canola)

1 TB. apple cider vinegar

1½ cups cooked beets, sliced

¼ medium red onion, thinly sliced

2 mandarin oranges, peeled and split into sections

1. In a medium bowl, whisk together orange juice, mustard, oil, and vinegar. Toss beets and onions in the mixture.

2. Cover and let marinate in the fridge for at least 8 hours.

3. When ready to serve, toss with mandarin slices. Store leftovers in the fridge for up to 5 days. The longer it sits, the more the flavors meld and the milder the flavor of the beets.

note

If your kiddo doesn't mind stronger flavors, serve this salad with crumbled goat cheese, feta, or even blue cheese. You can also toss it with peppery arugula or sweet baby spinach.

preparing beets

You can buy organic, cooked beets in your produce section, or you can roast them yourself. To roast beets, preheat oven to 350°F (180°C). Scrub unpeeled beets and cut into 2- to 3-inch (5–7.5cm) slices. Toss with olive oil and fold into a foil packet. Place foil packet on a baking sheet and roast for 1 hour. Cool and rub skins off with a paper towel.

easy barbecue chicken

This is one of our go-to recipes. You can use chicken thighs straight from the freezer, and at the end of the day, you have juicy barbecue chicken. Serve it to kiddos in a veggie-packed barbecue chicken quesadilla or toss it on a big bed of greens with quesadilla fixings for grown-ups.

PREP	5 minutes
COOK	4 to 8 hours
YIELD	4 cups
SERVING SIZE	2 tablespoons
SPECIAL TOOL	slow cooker

1 lb. (450g) boneless, skinless chicken thighs, frozen or fresh

1½ to 2 cups barbecue sauce

1. Combine chicken and barbecue sauce in a medium slow cooker. If frozen, cook on low for 7 to 8 hours. If fresh, cook on low for 4 hours.

2. One hour before serving, shred chicken to help it soak in all the barbecue goodness.

3. Store leftovers in the fridge in an airtight container for up to 4 days.

variation

To make **Easy Marinara Chicken,** replace the barbeque sauce with marinara sauce. Serve it over whole-wheat spaghetti noodles or toss it with shredded mozzarella and cook it like a quesadilla.

barbecue chicken quesadillas

To make our favorite veggie-packed barbecue chicken quesadillas, combine 3 TB. barbecue chicken, 1 TB. sliced red onion, 1 TB. corn, 1 TB. shredded zucchini, 1 TB. shredded carrot, 1 TB. diced avocado, and 3 TB. shredded cheese in a small bowl. Spread filling on one half of a whole-wheat tortilla. Fold over and cook in a dry frying pan for 4 minutes, flip and cook for 1 minute, and then flip again and cook for an additional 30 seconds to 1 minute, until outside is crispy and cheese is melted.

crispy baked potato fries

There aren't many recipes that actually benefit from prepping ahead of time, but this is one of them. You can slice the potatoes up to 24 hours before you plan to use them, then all you have to do is dry them off, throw them in a bag, add seasonings, and shake—or even better, have your toddler shake the bag. Throw them in the oven and voilà! Crispy fries!

PREP	10 minutes, plus 1 to 24 hours re-frigeration
COOK	35 to 45 minutes
YIELD	35 to 45 fries
SERVING SIZE	3 to 4 fries

2 medium potatoes	1 TB. olive or grapeseed oil	½ to 1 tsp. salt

1. Scrub potatoes and cut into ½-inch (1.25cm) slices. If you like meatier fries, cut them thicker. For crispier fries, cut them thinner.

2. Place potatoes in a medium bowl and cover with water. Refrigerate for 1 to 24 hours.

3. When ready to bake, preheat the oven to 450°F (230°C). Line a baking sheet with parchment paper.

4. Remove potatoes from water and dry thoroughly. Place in a large zipper-lock bag. Pour in oil and add salt. Seal and shake well to coat potatoes.

5. Spread potatoes on prepared pan in an even layer. Bake for 20 minutes and flip. Bake for an additional 15 to 25 minutes, depending on how crispy you want your fries. Serve immediately.

variation

For **Sweet Potato Fries,** use sweet potatoes instead of regular potatoes, and add ¼ teaspoon ground cinnamon and ¼ teaspoon sugar.

very veggie lasagna

This lasagna comes together quickly and is full of nutrient-rich veggies. The soft noodles and variety of textures are perfect for little mouths.

PREP	30 minutes
COOK	60 minutes
YIELD	1 (9×11-inch; 23×28cm) pan or 2 8×8-inch (20×20cm) pans
SERVING SIZE	1 2×2-inch (5×5cm) slice

1 tsp. olive oil

1 medium onion, diced

1 lb. (450g) grass-fed ground beef

1½ (24-oz.; 680g) jars marinara sauce

1 tsp. ground nutmeg

¼ tsp. salt

¼ tsp. ground pepper

1 cup shredded carrots

1 cup sliced mushrooms

1 cup thawed frozen broccoli or lightly steamed broccoli

1 cup reduced-fat cottage cheese

1 cup reduced-fat ricotta cheese

2 TB. Italian seasoning

6 no-boil lasagna noodles

2 cups fresh spinach

2 cups mozzarella cheese, shredded

1. In a medium frying pan over medium-high heat, sauté the onion in the oil until softened, approximately 2 to 3 minutes. Add the ground beef and cook until browned. Drain any excess fat.

2. Add ½ jar marinara, ground nutmeg, salt, and pepper.

3. In a medium bowl, combine carrots, mushrooms, and broccoli.

4. In another medium bowl, combine ricotta cheese, cottage cheese, and Italian seasoning.

5. Spread ½ jar marinara on the bottom of a 9×11-inch (23×28cm) pan. Place 3 noodles on top of sauce in a single layer. Spread ½ of the meat mixture on top of the noodles. Next, add ½ of the cheese mixture followed by 1 cup spinach, and then ½ of the veggie mixture.

6. Repeat the layers with the remaining ingredients: noodles, meat, cheese, spinach, and veggies. On top of the veggies, spread an additional ½ jar of the marinara. Sprinkle mozzarella cheese evenly on top.

7. Cover pan with foil and bake for 40 minutes. Remove the foil and bake for an additional 15 to 20 minutes until cheese is melted and bubbly. Let sit for at least 10 minutes before cutting.

8. Store leftovers in the fridge for up to 5 days or in the freezer for up to 1 month.

make ahead

The whole dish can be prepped up to 1 day in advance. Make it during naptime to make dinnertime a breeze. You can also freeze the lasagna. To reheat from frozen, double the baking time, or thaw and bake as directed.

12 to 17 months

vegetable-packed meatloaf

PREP	15 minutes
COOK	75 to 90 minutes
YIELD	2 large loaves
SERVING SIZE	1 slice

My daughter doesn't like meat and she doesn't like vegetables, but for some reason, she will eat this meatloaf. If your little one has no trouble eating vegetables, then feel free to halve all the veggies. You will still have a very healthy meatloaf. But if you're desperate to get some veggies into your little one, here is your vehicle.

variation

To make **Egg-Free Meatloaf,** replace eggs and oats with 2 pieces of whole-wheat bread soaked in whole milk. Start soaking bread before you prep the vegetables and then add to the rest of the ingredients, being careful to break up the bread and distribute throughout the mixture.

1 lb. (450 g) ground pork

1 lb. (450 g) grass-fed ground beef

2 cups fresh spinach, chopped

1 cup shredded carrots, roughly chopped

1 cup zucchini, finely diced

½ cup onion, diced (approximately 1 medium onion)

2 large eggs

1 cup rolled oats

½ cup ketchup

¼ cup yellow mustard

1 tsp. ground black pepper

½ tsp. salt

½ tsp. chili powder

1. Preheat oven to 350°F (180°C). Line a rimmed baking sheet with foil.

2. In a large bowl, combine all the ingredients. Use your hands to mix ingredients until well incorporated. It may take a while to get it together, but try not to overmix.

3. Divide meat mixture in half and form two loaves on the prepared sheet. Bake for 75 to 90 minutes until meat is cooked through. Let sit for 10 minutes and then serve. Leftovers can be refrigerated in an airtight container for up to 5 days.

note

This is a great make-ahead meal. Prep it during naptime (or the night before) and then throw it into the oven at dinnertime. You can also freeze the unbaked loaves. Thaw completely and then bake as directed.

For speedier cooking, bake at 375°F (190°C) for 50 to 60 minutes. This will result in a pink center, but if you save those sections for leftovers, the meat will cook fully when reheated and stay moist.

barbecue tofu

Tofu is a great, easy protein to make for your little one. This recipe can be a fast lunch or dressed up for a week-night dinner. You can either use store-bought barbecue sauce (just keep an eye out for high-fructose corn syrup), or you can throw together this sauce with some pantry staples and avoid the spicy kick that can be hard on sensitive young taste buds. Serve with corn and diced avocado.

PREP	10 minutes
COOK	15 minutes
YIELD	28 to 32 triangles
SERVING SIZE	3 to 4 triangles

⅓ cup ketchup

2 TB. yellow mustard

1 TB. brown sugar, packed

1 TB. soy sauce

1 TB. water

1 (10-oz.; 285g) package firm or extra firm tofu, cut into small triangles

1. Preheat oven to 450°F (230°C). Line a baking sheet with foil.

2. In a small bowl, whisk together ketchup, mustard, brown sugar, soy sauce, and water.

3. Place tofu triangles on prepared pan. Use a basting brush to brush on sauce. Apply thickly.

4. Bake for 8 minutes. Remove pan and brush another layer of sauce on the tofu. Bake for 3 more minutes, and brush with more sauce. Repeat twice. Let cool and serve immediately. Store leftovers in the fridge for up to 5 days.

tip
Serve cold leftover triangles as a healthy, protein-packed snack.

mac 'n' greens

PREP	5 minutes
COOK	15 minutes
YIELD	3 to 4 cups
SERVING SIZE	1/3 cup

tip

You will get the best results if you grate your own cheese. Pre-shredded cheese has anti-caking agents to keep the shreds from clumping. Those same additives prevent you from getting ooey-gooey, creamy macaroni and cheese.

The key to this recipe is overcooking the noodles so they are soft and easy for little mouths to break down. The goat cheese and tofu may seem out of place, but they both serve important functions. The tofu adds body (and protein) without having to use heavy cream, and the goat cheese gives it the tang of a certain orange-colored sauce favored by kids everywhere. This is a one-pot dish, perfect for quick weekday meals.

1 qt. (1l) water

Pinch salt

1 cup uncooked whole-wheat elbow noodles

2 cups broccoli florets

1/2 cup shredded carrots, optional

1 cup baby spinach

1 cup frozen peas, optional

1/4 cup whole milk

1 (6-oz.; 170g) package silken or firm tofu

3/4 tsp. ground mustard

1/4 tsp. ground nutmeg

3 TB. unsalted butter

1 cup grated cheddar cheese

1 TB. goat cheese

Pinch ground black pepper

1. In a medium saucepan, bring salted water to boil over high heat. Add noodles, broccoli florets, and shredded carrots. Cook for 8 minutes (or 1 minute longer than the directions on the pasta box). Add spinach and peas and cook for an additional minute.

2. Meanwhile, combine milk, tofu, ground mustard, and ground nutmeg in a blender. Purée until smooth.

3. Drain the noodles and veggies in a colander. Reduce heat to low. Return pan to stove and melt butter. Add veggies and noodles back to the pan. Add milk mixture and stir to combine. Add cheddar and goat cheese. Stir until the cheese is melted.

4. Top with freshly ground pepper and serve immediately.

5. Leftovers can be kept in a sealed container in the fridge for up to 5 days or in the freezer for up to 1 month. Reheat in a saucepan over medium heat with a splash of milk and a sprinkle of freshly grated cheese. Stir frequently.

substitutions

Don't like goat cheese? Blue cheese will give you a similar tang. If you think your little one will be overwhelmed with the veggies, you can take them out or limit them to veggies you know she likes.

sloppy josephines

PREP	10 to 15 minutes
COOK	20 to 25 minutes
YIELD	5 to 6 cups
SERVING SIZE	¼ cup

Who knew Sloppy Joes could be so healthy? By packing in a ton of vegetables, this is a comfort food you can feel good about feeding your family. It freezes well, so it's a great meal for stocking your freezer. For summer parties, you can double or triple this recipe and serve with nacho toppings. It's easy and always a crowd pleaser.

1 TB. grapeseed or canola oil	2 medium carrots, peeled and diced	¾ cup ketchup
1 sweet red, yellow, or orange pepper, ribs and seeds removed, diced	1 cup sliced mushrooms, diced	¼ cup yellow mustard
	1 lb. (450g) grass-fed ground beef	1 TB. brown sugar, packed
1 medium onion, diced	¼ tsp. salt	1 cup water
3 ribs celery, diced	¼ tsp. ground black pepper	

1. In a large frying pan, heat oil over medium-high heat. Add pepper, onion, carrot, celery, and mushrooms. Cook until softened, about 5 minutes.

2. Add beef. Season with salt and pepper. Break apart and cook until brown. Drain fat.

3. Add ketchup, mustard, water, and brown sugar. Stir to combine. Reduce heat to low and simmer for 5 minutes.

4. Serve immediately. Refrigerate in an airtight container for up to 5 days or store in the freezer for up to 3 months.

variations

For **Sloppy G's**, add 1 (15-oz.; 420g) can of rinsed and drained chickpeas to the sauce in step 3.

For **Sloppy Vinnies**, replace meat with 1 (15-oz.; 420g) can kidney beans, rinsed and drained; 1 (15-oz.; 420g) can black beans, rinsed and drained; 1 (14.5-oz.; 411g) can diced tomatoes, and 1 (15.25-oz.; 432g) can corn, rinsed and drained.

12 to 17 months

chicken *enchiladas*

The taste and texture of enchiladas are great for little mouths. If you don't have the time or the patience to roll up the enchiladas, simply layer sauce, tortillas (torn into quarters), and filling in the pan. Top with cheese and you're ready to go!

PREP	25 to 30 minutes
COOK	30 minutes
YIELD	1 9×13-inch (23×33cm) pan
SERVING SIZE	½ cup or 1 enchilada

4 cups Mexican Chicken (see sidebar)

1 cup frozen corn

1 (15-oz.; 420g) can black beans or 1 ½ cups cooked black beans

1 to 1½ cups shredded cheddar cheese

3 cups Homemade Enchilada Sauce (see sidebar) or 2 (14-oz.; 400g) cans enchilada sauce

14 to 16 4-inch (10cm) corn tortillas

1. Preheat oven to 375°F (190°C).

2. In a large bowl, combine Mexican Chicken, corn, black beans, and ½ cup shredded cheese.

3. Pour 1½ cups Enchilada Sauce in a 9×13-inch (23×33cm) cake pan.

4. Wrap 2 corn tortillas in a damp paper towel and microwave for 10 seconds to soften. Place 2 TB. filling in 1 tortilla, roll, and place in the pan, seam side down. Continue softening and filling tortillas until you have filled the pan, approximately 14 to 16 tortillas.

5. Pour the remaining 1½ cups Homemade Enchilada Sauce over rolled tortillas. Cover with remaining ½ to 1 cup cheese.

6. Bake 25 to 30 minutes until cheese is melted and cooked through, then broil for 4 to 6 minutes until cheese is browned and bubbly. Let sit 10 minutes before serving. Store leftovers in the fridge for up to 5 days.

mexican chicken

To make **Mexican Chicken,** add 1 lb. (450g) frozen boneless, skinless chicken thighs to a medium slow cooker. Pour 1 (15.5-oz.; 425g) jar salsa over the top. Cook on low for 8 to 10 hours; shred the chicken before the last hour of cooking.

homemade enchilada sauce

To make a quick and easy **Homemade Enchilada Sauce**, preheat broiler and line a rimmed baking sheet with foil. Peel and wash 1½ lbs. (680g) tomatillos and cut in half. Peel 1 medium onion and cut in half. Peel 3 cloves of garlic. Remove stems and seeds from 2 poblano peppers. Place all ingredients on prepared baking sheet, cut side down. Broil 6 to 8 minutes until charred and soft to the touch. Purée ingredients in a blender with ¼ cup fresh cilantro and juice of 1 large lime.

tomato and black bean *enchiladas*

Enchiladas are a great food for new eaters. They are soft and packed with flavor, and you can sneak a lot of healthy foods into them. You can prep them during naptime and put them in the oven whenever you're ready to eat. This recipe was born out of what I could find in my pantry. It comes together quickly and reheats easily, making it a great dish to have on hand for babysitters or busy nights.

PREP	20 minutes
COOK	30 minutes
YIELD	1 8×8-inch (20×20cm) pan
SERVING SIZE	½ cup or 1 enchilada

1 medium sweet potato, scrubbed

1½ cups cooked black beans or 1 (15-oz.; 425g) can black beans, rinsed and drained

1 (10-oz.; 250ml) can enchilada sauce (green or red)

3 TB. tomato paste

8 to 9 6-inch (15cm) corn tortillas

³⁄₄ tsp. cumin

¼ to ½ tsp. chili powder (optional)

1¼ cup shredded cheddar

1. Preheat oven to 350°F (180°C).

2. Poke holes in sweet potato with a fork. Microwave on high for 5 to 6 minutes until fork-tender.

3. Meanwhile, mash black beans in a large bowl with a potato masher until at least half of beans are mashed.

4. When sweet potato is done, cut in half and scoop the flesh from the skin. Mash with black beans until well combined. Add tomato paste and mash to combine. Add cumin, chili powder (if using), and ½ cup cheese. Stir to combine.

5. Pour ½ can enchilada sauce into an 8×8-inch (20×20cm) baking dish. Take two corn tortillas and wrap them in a damp paper towel. Microwave on high for 10 seconds to soften.

6. Spread 2 TB. filling down the middle of a tortilla. Wrap the tortilla around the filling and place it seam side down in the prepared pan. Continue warming and filling the remaining tortillas.

7. Pour remaining ½ can enchilada sauce over the tortillas. Cover with remaining ³⁄₄ cup shredded cheese. Bake for 25 minutes.

8. Turn on the broiler and broil for 2 to 3 minutes until cheese is brown and bubbly.

9. Let stand for 10 minutes before serving. Serve with shredded lettuce, salsa, guacamole, and sour cream or Greek yogurt. Keep leftovers in the fridge for up to 5 days.

squash *soup*

PREP	10 minutes
COOK	5 to 6 hours
YIELD	7 cups
SERVING SIZE	1/3 cup
SPECIAL TOOLS	slow cooker

nutritional note

Butternut squash is rich in vitamin A. This is a very important nutrient for children. It helps your kiddo's eyes and bones develop. It's also great for their immune systems.

It's been an uphill battle for me to find the perfect squash soup recipe. Most soups are too sweet, so I worked hard to add some savory elements. I have some tricks for prepping the squash so you don't have to deal with the mess of scooping out roasted squash or worry about losing a finger. The cooking time may seem long, but most of it is in the slow cooker.

1 medium or 2 small butternut squash

4 2-inch (5cm) sprigs fresh rosemary

1 to 2 TB. unsalted butter

2 green apples, peeled and diced

2 medium onions, peeled and chopped

4 cups vegetable broth

1/4 tsp. white ground pepper

1/4 tsp. ground cinnamon

1/2 tsp. garam masala

1 tsp. salt

2 TB. brown sugar

1. Preheat oven to 400°F (200°C).

2. Use a vegetable peeler to peel the squash. Cut the ends off the squash and then cut in half. Scoop out the seeds.

3. Place squash halves in a square cake pan, scooped side up. Spread 1/2 TB. butter in the cavity and neck of each squash half and line with rosemary sprigs. Bake for 60 to 75 minutes until the squash is fork-tender. Remove rosemary sprigs.

4. In a medium slow cooker, combine squash, apples, onion, vegetable broth, white pepper, cinnamon, garam masala, salt, and brown sugar. Cook on high for 4 hours.

5. Use an immersion blender to purée the soup. You can also blend the soup in two batches in a regular blender. Cover with a towel instead of the blender lid so the hot air can escape. Serve immediately.

6. Refrigerate in an airtight container for up to 1 week or freeze for up to 3 months.

spaghetti *sauce*

This is a quick and easy spaghetti sauce you can throw together while the pasta cooks. I love adding a lot of veggies to my sauce. You may want to chop the veggies super fine, depending on your kiddo's comfort level. Some people advocate puréeing the sauce to "hide" the veggies, but if you leave them in chunks, it will help your kiddo get used to having veggies in her sauce.

PREP	10 minutes
COOK	10 to 15 minutes
YIELD	4 to 5 cups
SERVING SIZE	1/3 cup

1 TB. olive oil

1/2 medium onion, diced

1/2 cup shredded carrots, chopped

1/2 green pepper, diced

1 cup sliced mushrooms, chopped

1/2 tsp. minced garlic

1 (26-oz.; 737g) carton strained tomatoes or 1 (28-oz.; 794g) can puréed tomatoes

1 TB. Italian seasoning

2 tsp. balsamic vinegar

1/4 tsp. salt

1/4 tsp. ground black pepper

1. In a large frying pan with high sides, heat oil over medium-high heat. Add onion, carrots, pepper, and mushrooms. Cook until softened, about 2 to 3 minutes. Add garlic and cook for 30 seconds or until fragrant.

2. Add strained tomatoes, Italian seasoning, balsamic vinegar, salt, and pepper. Reduce heat to low and simmer for 5 to 10 minutes, stirring occasionally.

3. Serve immediately. Leftovers can be refrigerated in an airtight container for up to 5 days or kept frozen for up to 3 months.

variation

For a **Meat Sauce,** reduce mushrooms to 1/2 cup and add 1 lb. (450g) grass-fed ground beef after the garlic. Drain the fat and then add the remaining ingredients. You could also add 2 to 3 sliced, pre-cooked Italian sausages.

12 to 17 months

all-natural microwave popcorn

PREP	5 minutes
COOK	1 to 3 minutes
YIELD	2 to 3 cups
SERVING SIZE	½ cup
SPECIAL TOOLS	1 brown paper lunch bag

Popcorn is a great, whole-grain snack for little hands and little mouths. Using a simple brown paper lunch bag, you can make your own popcorn without any chemical additives or even oil. It's economical, too—purchasing popcorn kernels is much less expensive than buying boxes of microwave popcorn, and the results are just as quick and tasty.

¼ cup popcorn kernels   Seasoning of your choice (see sidebar)

1. Place ¼ cup unpopped popcorn kernels in a brown paper lunch bag. Fold over the top of the bag about ½ inch (1.25cm) and then fold again. Place bag in microwave, folded edge down.

2. Microwave on high for 1½ to 3 minutes. Listen carefully and stop as soon as the popping starts to slow down. Serve immediately.

note
Microwaves vary in strength, so you may need to adjust the power settings or timing.

spice it up
Little ones may not need any extra flavor, but you may want something more. Here are some of our favorite flavorings. Simply add the oil and seasonings right in the bag after it's popped, shake, and pour into a bowl.

Classic: 1 TB. olive or grapeseed oil + ¼ tsp. salt

Spicy: 1 TB. olive or grapeseed oil + ¼ tsp. salt + ¼ tsp. ground black pepper + 1 to 3 dashes hot sauce

Sweet: 1 TB. melted butter + ½ tsp. ground cinnamon + ½ to 1 tsp. sugar

Cheesy: 1 TB. olive or grapeseed oil + ½ tsp. nutritional yeast + ¼ tsp. salt

Try your favorite herbs, spices, and oils to customize to your taste buds!

homemade hummus

PREP	15 minutes
YIELD	2 cups
SERVING SIZE	1 to 2 tablespoons
SPECIAL TOOLS	food processor

My family devours hummus, so it's no surprise that making my own has become an obsession. I've tried everything from shelling every chickpea to grinding my own sesame seeds. Both are a complete waste of time. If I only knew it was just a matter of time—specifically time spent puréeing. If you purée the chickpeas for a full 10 minutes, you will be rewarded with the creamiest hummus you could ever imagine.

3 TB. tahini

Juice of 1 large lemon (about ¼ cup)

1 small clove garlic

3 TB. olive oil

¼ tsp. paprika

½ tsp. salt

1 (15-oz.; 425g) can chickpeas, rinsed and drained or 1½ cups cooked chickpeas

note

Because of the long purée time, I do not recommend using a blender as it may heat the hummus.

1. In a food processor fitted with a chopping blade, combine lemon juice and tahini. Process for 1 minute. Scrape down sides with a spatula as necessary.

2. Add garlic, olive oil, paprika, and salt. Process for 1 minute. Scrape down the sides with a spatula as necessary.

3. Add ½ can chickpeas. Process for 5 minutes. Scrape down the sides with a spatula as necessary.

4. Add remaining ½ can chickpeas. Process for 5 minutes. Scrape down the sides with a spatula as necessary. Serve immediately or save for later.

5. Hummus can be stored in an airtight container in the fridge for up to 1 week.

variation

For **Roasted Red Pepper Hummus,** make hummus as directed. After puréeing the chickpeas, add ½ cup jarred roasted red peppers and purée until fully combined, 30 seconds to 1 minute.

baby guacamole

This is a super-easy spread to throw together and is made with pantry staples. Serve on a whole-wheat tortilla, whole-wheat toast, or as a dip for veggies or whole-grain crackers. The olive oil makes it extra creamy and the balsamic vinegar gives it a tangy sweetness that is milder than the traditional lime juice.

PREP	5 minutes
YIELD	1/2 cup
SERVING SIZE	1 to 2 tablespoons

1 ripe avocado, peeled and pitted

2 TB. salsa
1 dash balsamic vinegar

1 dash olive oil

1. In a small bowl, mash avocado with the salsa and oil. Stir in the balsamic vinegar. Serve immediately.

2. Store leftovers in the fridge for up to 1 day. To keep the guacamole from turning brown, cover with a piece of plastic wrap and press it into the surface of the guacamole.

nutritional note

Avocados are a nutritional powerhouse filled with good fats and rich in antioxidants, vitamin E, vitamin C, fiber, and folate.

12 to 17 months

black bean *dip*

Black beans are a great source of fiber and protein. By adding some sweet carrots and zesty salsa, you have a flavorful and healthy dip for your little one. You could serve it with veggies, but since the dip is so healthy, I have no qualms about serving it with crackers or baked tortilla chips.

PREP	10 minutes
YIELD	2 cups
SERVING SIZE	1 to 2 tablespoons
SERVING SIZE	food processor

1 (15-oz.; 425g) can black beans, rinsed and drained or 1 1/2 cup cooked black beans, rinsed and drained

1 carrot, peeled and grated (approximately 1/4 cup)

2 TB. salsa

1/4 tsp. smoked paprika

1/4 tsp. ground cumin

1/4 tsp. chili powder

Juice of 2 limes (approximately 3 TB.)

1/2 TB. oil, grapeseed or olive

1. In a food processor fitted with a chopping blade, combine all ingredients. Process until smooth.

2. Store in an airtight container in the fridge for up to 5 days.

note

If you are buying canned black beans, look for cans with BPA-free linings. Some brands are starting to package black beans in cartons, which are also BPA free. And, of course, you can always make them from dried.

12 to 17 months

make your own tortilla chips

To make your own tortilla chips, tear corn tortillas into quarters. Spread in an even layer on a rimmed baking sheet and spray with oil spray. Sprinkle salt on top and bake at 350°F (180°C) for 20 minutes until crisp, rotating pan halfway through cooking time. Serve immediately. Store leftovers in an airtight container for up to 1 day.

three-ingredient cheese crackers

PREP	10 minutes, plus 1 hour to 3 days to chill the dough
COOK	15 to 17 minutes
YIELD	40 to 45 crackers
SERVING SIZE	2 to 3 crackers
SPECIAL TOOLS	food processor

I first learned of these magic crackers from Lisa Leake's blog, *100 Days of Real Food.* I tweaked her recipe a little to make it more palatable for toddlers. To make life even easier, I freeze 1½-cup portions of shredded cheese in zipper-lock bags, so I can just pull a bag out in the morning and have it measured and ready for naptime cooking. These are my go-to diaper bag staple.

1 cup whole-wheat pastry flour

1½ cups shredded cheese

5 TB. unsalted butter, cold and cut into cubes

1. In a food processor fitted with a chopping blade, combine whole-wheat pastry flour, cheese, and butter. Turn processor on and keep it running until dough forms a ball. This may take a few minutes.

2. Place the dough on a large piece of wax paper. Use your hands to form dough into a log, approximately 1½ to 2 inches (4–5cm) in diameter. The size of the log will determine the size of the crackers. Wrap dough in wax paper and refrigerate for at least 1 hour and up to 3 days. If the dough is in the fridge for over 1 day, let it sit at room temperature for 5 to 10 minutes.

3. Preheat oven to 350°F (180°C).

4. Cut dough into slices, ranging from ¼ inch to ½ inch (6–12mm) thick. The thicker the slice, the more cookie-like the cracker. Place on an ungreased baking sheet.

5. Bake for 15 to 17 minutes until crackers are set and beginning to darken on the edges.

6. Transfer crackers from baking sheet onto a wire rack and let cool completely.

7. Store in a covered container at room temperature for 2 to 3 days or freeze in zipper-lock bags for up to 1 month.

variations

To make **Cheddar and Chive Crackers,** add 3 TB. chopped chives to the other ingredients.

To make **Sun-Dried Tomato Crackers,** place 2 TB. sliced sun-dried tomatoes in the food processor before you add the other ingredients. Pulse until finely chopped and then continue.

wheat crackers

With no mess to your kitchen and only 10 minutes, you can make your own wheat crackers. This recipe was modified from the King Arthur Flour recipe for wheat crackers. The spelt flour gives it a sweet, nutty taste, while the white pepper adds just the right amount of zing.

1¼ cup spelt flour
1½ TB. sugar
½ tsp. salt

¼ tsp. white ground pepper
4 TB. unsalted butter, cold and cut into cubes

¼ cup ice cold water

PREP	10 minutes
COOK	15 minutes
YIELD	32 to 40 crackers
SERVING SIZE	2 to 3 crackers
SPECIAL TOOLS	food processor

1. Preheat oven to 350°F (180°C).

2. In a food processor fitted with a chopping blade, add spelt flour, sugar, salt, and white pepper. Pulse until combined. Add butter and pulse until mixture has small crumbs.

3. Turn on processor and add ice water one tablespoon at a time, pausing after each addition. Add water until dough becomes a ball (this will likely require ¼ cup ice water).

4. Place a piece of parchment paper on the counter. Place half of the dough on the parchment paper and use your hands to flatten into a disc. Sprinkle with flour, and roll out as thin as you can. You may need to add additional flour to keep it from sticking to the rolling pin.

5. Use a pizza cutter to cut into 2×3-inch (5×8cm) rectangles. Do not separate. Transfer the parchment paper to a baking sheet. Bake for 5 minutes.

6. Remove from oven and separate crackers. You may need to recut using a metal spatula or a pizza cutter. Bake for an additional 5 to 10 minutes. If your crackers are a little thicker, they may need more than 5 minutes. The crackers are done when golden and brown around the edges.

7. Transfer parchment paper to a metal cooling rack and allow to cool completely. Store in an airtight container for up to 3 days or in the freezer for up to 1 month.

note

The spelt flour gives the crackers a nutty taste reminiscent of Wheat Thins. You could use whole-wheat pastry flour, but it will not have that nutty flavor.

12 to 17 months

wheat crackers | 139

cinnamon graham crackers

These crackers are a diaper bag staple. Unlike commercially made graham crackers, these won't crumble and make a mess. They have all of the nutty taste of graham crackers without unnecessary additives.

PREP	15 minutes, plus at least 4 hours to chill the dough
BAKE	20 to 25 minutes
YIELD	30 crackers
SERVING SIZE	2 to 3 crackers
SPECIAL TOOLS	food processor

note

For a stronger cinnamon flavor, replace 2 tsp. cinnamon with 2 TB. cinnamon.

substitution

If your little one is under a year old, she should not have honey as it can cause infant botulism. Substitute maple syrup for honey. Do not use artificial maple syrup.

1½ cups whole-wheat pastry flour or white whole-wheat flour

1 cup spelt flour

½ cup dark brown sugar, packed

¾ tsp. salt

2 tsp. ground cinnamon

½ cup unsalted butter, cold and cut into cubes

¼ cup honey

½ cup milk or non-dairy milk

1 tsp. vanilla extract

1. In a food processor fitted with a chopping blade, pulse together whole-wheat pastry flour, spelt flour, brown sugar, salt, and cinnamon.

2. Add unsalted butter, and pulse until a coarse meal forms.

3. Add honey, milk, and vanilla extract, and pulse until dough is formed.

4. Divide dough in half. Form each half into a disc, approximately ½-inch (1.25cm) thick. Wrap each disc tightly in plastic wrap.

5. Refrigerate wrapped discs for at least 4 hours and up to 4 days.

6. Preheat oven to 350°F (180°C).

7. Place a piece of parchment paper on the counter. Unwrap one disc of dough and place the plastic wrap over the dough, so it is sandwiched between the parchment and plastic wrap. Roll out to ¼-inch to ⅛-inch (3-6mm) thickness.

8. Use a pizza cutter to cut into 2×3-inch (5×7.5cm) rectangles. Do not separate. Transfer the parchment paper to a baking sheet. Bake for 15 minutes. While first pan is baking, roll out the second disc of dough.

9. Remove from oven and separate crackers. You may need to recut using a metal spatula or a pizza cutter. Bake for an additional 5 minutes.

10. Transfer parchment paper to a metal cooling rack. Cool completely. Store in a covered container for up to 4 days or in the freezer for up to 3 months.

Use a pizza cutter to cut dough into rectangles (step 8).

After baking 15 minutes, separate crackers (step 9).

blueberry banana *bread*

PREP	15 minutes
COOK	50 to 60 minutes
YIELD	1 loaf
SERVING SIZE	½ slice

note

To make 12 muffins, grease a 12-cup muffin pan and bake for 25 to 30 minutes.

Bananas and blueberries come together in this sweet but healthy and moist bread. I like to think of them as in a yin and yang for babies' digestion: blueberries keep them regular and bananas keep things solid. Together, they balance each other out. The blueberries add sweetness and color to the otherwise drab banana bread.

2½ cups whole-wheat pastry flour

½ tsp. ground cinnamon

1 tsp. baking soda

1 tsp. baking powder

⅛ tsp. salt

½ cup fresh blueberries or frozen blueberries, thawed

3 ripe bananas, peeled and smashed (about 1¾ cups)

½ cup unsweetened applesauce

½ cup sugar

1 large egg

1 tsp. vanilla extract

1. Preheat oven to 350°F (180°C). Grease a 9×5×3-inch (23×12.5×7.5cm) loaf pan.

2. In a medium bowl, whisk together whole-wheat pastry flour, ground cinnamon, baking soda, baking powder, and salt with a fork. Fold in blueberries with a wooden spoon and stir until berries are coated with flour.

3. In a large bowl, mash bananas with applesauce. Add sugar, egg, and vanilla extract.

4. Add flour mixture to banana mixture and stir until just combined. Pour batter into prepared pan.

5. Bake 50 to 60 minutes, until toothpick inserted in center of loaf comes out clean.

6. Let cool in pan on cooling rack for 15 to 20 minutes. Run a butter knife around the edges, and invert loaf on the rack to cool completely.

7. Store wrapped in aluminum foil in the fridge for 3 to 5 days or in the freezer for up to 2 months.

cheddar apple *bread*

This bread is a great little afternoon snack. Packed with cheddar cheese and green apples, it hits both the sweet and savory notes.

PREP	15 minutes
COOK	40 to 45 minutes
YIELD	1 loaf
SERVING SIZE	½ slice

1 cup whole-wheat pastry flour

¾ cup whole-wheat flour

1 tsp. salt

¼ tsp. paprika

3 large eggs

⅓ cup milk

⅓ cup applesauce

1½ cups shredded cheddar cheese

1 green apple, finely diced

1. Preheat oven to 350°F (180°C). Grease a 9×5×3-inch (23×12.5×7.5cm) loaf pan.

2. In a large bowl, whisk together whole-wheat pastry flour, whole-wheat flour, salt, and paprika with a fork.

3. In a medium bowl, whisk together eggs, milk, and applesauce. Pour into the dry ingredients, and stir with a spatula until just combined.

4. Fold in cheese and apples. Pour batter into prepared pan. Bake for 40 to 45 minutes, until a toothpick inserted in center of loaf comes out clean.

5. Let cool in pan for 5 to 10 minutes on a cooling rack. Run a butter knife around the edges and invert onto rack to cool completely.

6. Store wrapped in aluminum foil in the fridge for 3 to 5 days or in the freezer for up to 2 months.

12 to 17 months

easy cream cheese frosting

1 (8-oz.; 225g) container reduced-fat cream cheese

3 TB. maple syrup or honey

1/3 cup Greek yogurt

3 TB. milk

In a large bowl, combine cream cheese, maple syrup, and Greek yogurt. Beat with an electric hand mixer on medium speed until well combined. Reduce speed to low and slowly add milk; blend until well combined. Chill for at least 1 hour before using.

first birthday cake

Here is a cake that will make everyone at your party happy. Yes, it is made with whole-grain flour, apple-sauce, and Greek yogurt, but the taste is pure ooey-gooey chocolate goodness. The cream cheese frosting is more tangy than sweet and the perfect canvas for chopped strawberries, mini chocolate chips, or sprinkles.

PREP	30 minutes
COOK	25 to 30 minutes
YIELD	1 (9×13-inch; 23×33cm) cake, or 2 8-inch (20cm) cake pans
SERVING SIZE	1 piece

½ cup dark chocolate chips

½ cup unsalted butter

½ cup unsweetened applesauce

1 cup cocoa powder

1½ cups whole-wheat pastry flour

1½ tsp. baking powder

1 tsp. baking soda

¼ tsp. ground cinnamon

¼ tsp. ground nutmeg

1½ tsp. salt

4 large eggs, room temperature

2 tsp. vanilla extract

1 cup sugar

1 cup fat-free Greek yogurt

1. Grease a 9×13-inch (23×33cm) cake pan. Preheat the oven to 350°F (180°C).

2. In a small glass bowl, combine chocolate chips, butter, applesauce, and cocoa powder. Microwave on high for 20 seconds, stir, and repeat until chocolate is melted. Set aside.

3. In a medium bowl, whisk together whole-wheat pastry flour, baking powder, baking soda, cinnamon, nutmeg, and salt.

4. In a large bowl, whisk eggs until frothy. Add vanilla extract, and whisk to combine. Whisk in sugar, followed by chocolate mixture.

5. Slowly stir flour mixture into egg mixture.

6. Fold in Greek yogurt until combined, and pour batter into prepared pan.

7. Bake for 25 to 30 minutes until the middle springs back when touched, or a toothpick inserted in the center comes out with just 1 or 2 crumbs. Cool completely on a cooling rack before frosting.

8. If desired, frost with Easy Cream Cheese Frosting or your own favorite frosting. Store leftover cake in the fridge for up to 1 week.

note

If making a layer cake, let the two layers chill in the fridge for at least 24 hours before assembling and frosting.

protein-packed fruit pops

PREP	10 minutes
FREEZE	3 to 4 hours
YIELD	1½ cups, or 6 (2-oz.; 60ml) fruit pops
SERVING SIZE	1 pop
SPECIAL TOOLS	ice pop molds

These fruity ice pops have a creamy consistency and a protein punch thanks to the addition of silken tofu. If your kiddo, like mine, goes through a phase where she refuses to eat meat, these can be a good way to help ensure that she gets enough protein. The mango and blueberry bring natural sweetness without the need for added sugars, and the flaxseed provides an additional boost of omega-3 fats.

1 cup fresh mango, diced

½ cup frozen or fresh blueberries

6 oz. (170g) silken tofu

1 TB. ground flaxseed

1. Combine all ingredients in a blender and purée until smooth. Scoop into ice pop molds. Freeze for 3 to 4 hours.

2. Store in freezer for up to 1 month.

note

In order to get the nutritional benefits from flaxseed, they have to be ground. You can buy flax meal (ground flaxseed) in the organic or natural food department of most grocery stores. Store ground flaxseed in the freezer or the fridge.

fudge *pops*

I grew up on fudge pops. I would love for my daughter to enjoy the same chocolaty treat, but most store-bought versions are not very nutritious. This recipe is the solution. The avocado brings creaminess and thickness that you just can't get with dairy. It's also a healthy fat that is great for kiddos (and for parents). Sweetened with dates and maple syrup, this is a treat with no guilt.

PREP	10 minutes
FREEZE	3 to 4 hours
YIELD	1½ cups, or 6 (2-oz.; 60ml) fudge pops
SERVING SIZE	1 pop
SPECIAL TOOLS	ice pop molds

2 dates, pitted

½ avocado, not too ripe

3 TB. cocoa powder

1 cup full-fat coconut milk

1 TB. maple syrup or honey

1. Place dates in a small bowl and cover with hot water. Let sit for 5 minutes, then drain.

2. Place softened dates, avocado, cocoa powder, coconut milk, and maple syrup in blender. Blend until smooth and no chunks remain. Scoop mixture in ice pop molds. Freeze for 3 to 4 hours.

3. Store in freezer for up to 1 month.

variation

For **Chocolate Mousse,** instead of freezing, pour mixture in small ramekins and chill for 1 to 2 hours. You could also eat it immediately.

nutritional note

Avocados and coconut milk are full of healthy fats. It's essential that children get a good amount of healthy fats in their diet. These fats support brain and nervous system development, and help the body absorb important vitamins like A, D, E, and K.

part 6

18 to 24 months

At 18 months, your kiddo is ready for more grown-up food. She has most of her teeth in, and she's getting better at using utensils, which means you don't have to break up her food into tiny pieces as much. Instead, her meals look more like mini versions of your own. In this section you'll find recipes for favorite standbys like Chicken Nuggets and Fish Sticks, as well as fun new bites like Baked Falafel, Honey Mustard Green Beans, and Blueberry Doughnuts.

what baby is eating now: *toddler meals*

Not much has changed since the last stage. Your child is still sharing the same foods as the rest of the family, but now you can try more toddler-style meals. This means bigger bites and bolder flavors and textures.

The art of using a spoon and fork is still a work in progress, so it's completely normal to continue finger foods. Try offering both types of food at a meal—food to pick up and food to eat with a spoon or fork. This way your kiddo can practice using utensils without getting hungry or frustrated.

Desserts and Sweet Treats

Sweets are a normal part of life and it's wise to show your child how to incorporate them without going overboard. Here are some ideas to get started:

- A treat is only a treat if you have it once in a while. Don't keep desserts in your house regularly.

- Don't be a closet eater. If you are having a dessert, share some with your child or let him have his own little portion.

- When your child asks for more dessert, explain to him why it's not good to eat a lot of it. You can say something like "too much dessert will make your tummy hurt."

- Save treats for the end of the meal. This way he will fill up on the nutritious food first.

- Try not to use dessert as a punishment or reward. That can create unhealthy food beliefs and behaviors.

Busy Bodies

It can be hard to get your toddler to sit still for a meal. His tiny tummy fills up fast! Continue to offer three meals and two snacks each day to help him get the fuel he needs.

Try not to worry if your child wants to get up from the table after only a few bites. Trust that he's eating the amount right for him. It's normal for toddlers to eat well one day and not so well the next. In the end it all balances out, as long as you provide a variety of healthy foods at each meal.

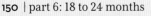

nutritional needs: 18 to 24 *months*

During this stage, weight gain continues to slow. You can expect your toddler to gain 5 to 8 ounces (140–225g) each month. Height will increase at the same rate of .3 inch (.75cm) per month.

It's common for parents of toddlers to worry about fat intake, but fat is an important nutrient in young children. According to the American Academy of Pediatrics, during the first two years of life, half of your child's calories should come from fat. The key is making sure the fat comes from healthy sources like lean meats, fatty fish, whole-milk dairy products, nuts, seeds, and avocado. Remember that your toddler has a small stomach. Here are approximate serving sizes for a child at this stage.

Food Group	Servings per Day	One Serving Equals
Grains	6	¼ slice of bread, ¼ cup cereal, rice or pasta, 1 or 2 crackers
Vegetables	3	1 TB. raw or cooked, ¼ cup leafy
Fruit	2 to 3	1 TB. pureed or canned, ¼ cup fresh
Dairy	2 to 3	4 oz. (100ml) milk, 1-inch (2.5cm) cube of cheese, 2 oz. (55g) yogurt
Protein	2	2 TB. ground meat or flaked fish, 1 egg, 2 TB. beans, 2 TB. nut butter

Nutritional Spotlight: Vitamin C

Vitamin C is an important nutrient for your child. It acts as an antioxidant, protecting his body from disease and environmental contaminants. Vitamin C is also used to build collagen, a strong protein found in bone, skin, and connective tissue.

Vitamin C is commonly found in fruits (especially citrus) and vegetables. Vitamin C can help your child absorb iron. If you're working on iron intake, it's helpful to pair iron-rich foods (like beef) with vitamin C–rich foods.

RECIPE TO TRY:
Roasted Broccoli and Cauliflower

foods rich in vitamin C

Bell peppers

Papaya

Broccoli

Brussels sprouts

Strawberries

Pineapple

Oranges

Grapefruit

Kiwi

Cantaloupe

Cauliflower

meal plans:
18 to 24 months

Here are daily and weekly meal plans for feeding your toddler at this stage. Keep in mind that every child is different. This is only meant to be a guide, not a strict schedule.

Sample Feeding Schedule

TIME	SLEEP AND FOOD
7:00 AM	Wake up for the day.
7:30 AM	Breakfast: protein (yogurt, egg) + fruit **or** whole grain + fruit
10:00 AM	Snack: fruit or veggie + milk **or** whole grain + milk
12:00 PM	Lunch: protein + veggie + starch
1:00 PM	Nap 1½ to 3 hours.
3:00 PM	Snack: fruit or veggie + milk **or** whole grain + milk
6:00 PM	Dinner: protein + veggie + starch
7:30 PM	Bedtime.

Meal Key

Protein = meat, beans, lentils, eggs, fish, yogurt, cheese

Starch = whole grains, potatoes, peas, winter squash (butternut, acorn), and corn

Veggie = any veggie other than potatoes, peas, winter squash, or corn

Sample Weekly Meal Plan

DAY	MEALS
Monday	**Breakfast:** ½ cup Pumpkin Pie Steel-Cut Oats **Snack:** ¼ cup chopped fresh mango + 4 oz. (110g) milk **Lunch:** 1 egg scrambled with spinach + ¼ piece of buttered toast **Snack:** 2 oz. (55g) Homemade Yogurt swirled with 3 TB. applesauce **Dinner:** 2 Chicken Nuggets + 3 Honey Mustard Green Beans + 4 oz. (110g) milk
Tuesday	**Breakfast:** ½ cup LO Pumpkin Pie Steel-Cut Oats **Snack:** ¼ cup banana slices + 4 oz. (110g) milk **Lunch:** 2 LO Chicken Nuggets and 3 Honey Mustard Green Beans **Snack:** 2 oz. (55g) Homemade Yogurt swirled with 3 TB. applesauce **Dinner:** 2 TB. Tofu Taco Filling + 4 baked tortilla chips + 4 oz. (110g) milk
Wednesday	**Breakfast:** 1 Banana Egg Pancake + 4 oz. (110g) milk **Snack:** ¼ cup applesauce with 1 tsp. ground or finely chopped walnuts **Lunch:** 1 baby quesadilla made with LO Tofu Taco Filling **Snack:** 3 steamed baby carrot sticks with Ranch Dip **Dinner:** 2 TB. Sloppy Josephine spooned over ½ bun cut into pieces + 2 TB. Roasted Broccoli and Cauliflower + 4 oz. (110g) milk
Thursday	**Breakfast:** ½ cup oatmeal with ¼ cup blueberries (fresh or frozen) **Snack:** ¼ cup chopped strawberries + 4 oz. (110g) milk **Lunch:** 2 TB. LO Sloppy Josephine spooned over ½ bun cut into pieces + 2 TB. LO Roasted Broccoli and Cauliflower + 4 oz. (110g) milk **Snack:** 3 steamed baby carrot sticks with Ranch Dip **Dinner:** 1 Baked Falafel patty with 1 TB. Cucumber Yogurt Sauce
Friday	**Breakfast:** ½ cup oatmeal with ¼ cup blueberries (fresh or frozen) **Snack:** ¼ cup chopped strawberries + 4 oz. (110g) milk **Lunch:** 1 LO Baked Falafel patty with 1 TB. LO Cucumber Yogurt Sauce **Snack:** 4 oz. (110g) Chocolate Peanut Butter Smoothie **Dinner:** 1-2 Fish Sticks + 2 TB. mashed potato + ¼ cup chopped green salad with Creamy Poppy Seed Vinaigrette
Saturday	**Breakfast:** ¼ Strawberry Waffle + 4 oz. (110g) milk **Snack:** 1 clementine (wedges cut in half) **Lunch:** ½ cup Squash Soup + 1 slice deli turkey spread with avocado, rolled and cut in half **Snack:** ½ piece of toast spread with peanut butter and cut into pieces + 4 oz. (110g) milk **Dinner:** 2 TB. Barbecue Chicken + 3 Crispy Baked Potato Fries + 1-2 TB. steamed broccoli
Sunday	**Breakfast:** ½ Make-Ahead Egg and Cheese Breakfast Sandwich **Snack:** 1 clementine (wedges cut in half)+ 4 oz. (110g) milk **Lunch:** LO Squash Soup + 1 slice deli turkey spread with avocado, rolled and cut in half **Snack:** ¼ cup chopped strawberries + 4 oz. (110g) milk **Dinner:** small slice of Vegetable-Packed Lasagna, cut into pieces

LO=leftover

make-ahead breakfast sandwiches

PREP	5 minutes
COOK	15 minutes
YIELD	8 sandwiches
SERVING SIZE	1/2 sandwich

On mornings after long nights, I rely on better mornings when I had the time and patience to make extra portions. These egg sandwiches can be a lifesaver and taste just like a fast-food egg sandwich, but better. By toasting the bread in the broiler while you cook the eggs in a skillet, you can have these ready in about 20 minutes.

8 English muffins, cut in half

3 TB. butter

8 large eggs

8 slices of cheddar cheese

8 slices of nitrate-free deli ham

1. Preheat broiler to high. Leave the oven door cracked open.

2. Place English muffin halves on baking sheet. They can overlap each other. Lightly spread butter on each muffin.

3. Heat an electric skillet or frying pan to medium-high heat. Spray with cooking spray. Crack eggs into pan. The whites can touch each other. Break the yolks using a spatula.

4. While eggs begin to cook, place English muffins in oven. Broil for 3 minutes and check on them. You may need to rotate the pan. Broil for an additional 2 minutes until golden brown.

5. While the English muffins are toasting, cook the eggs until the whites are set, and flip. You may need to use your spatula to cut between the eggs. Cook until yolk is cooked through. Make sure not to overcook the eggs.

6. Remove the eggs from the pan one at a time, using a thin metal spatula. Place a slice of cheese over each egg as it cools. Let it cool for 5 minutes.

7. Place a piece of ham on the bottom half of an English muffin. Cover with egg and cheese. Place of the top half of the English muffin on top. Repeat with all sandwiches. Let cool for 5 minutes.

make them your own

These sandwiches can easily be customized. Prefer sausage patties? Go for it. No meat? Leave it out. You can also make as many or as few sandwiches as you see fit. Just be sure to fry the eggs; scrambling or baking eggs will lead to a spongy, watery mess.

8. Wrap each sandwich tightly with two layers of plastic wrap. Place all sandwiches in a gallon-size zipper-lock freezer bag. Label bag with instructions on reheating. Store in the freezer for up to 1 month.

9. To reheat from frozen, microwave on high for 90 seconds. You can also thaw the sandwich in the fridge overnight and reheat on high for 60 seconds.

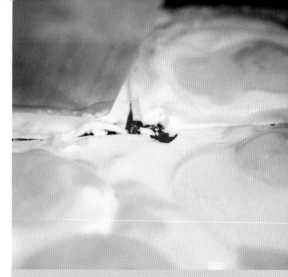

Separate eggs with a spatula if needed (step 5).

nut-free granola

PREP	10 minutes
COOK	40 to 50 minutes
YIELD	10 cups
SERVING SIZE	2 to 3 tablespoons

Since so many kids have nut allergies, I wanted to create a granola for everyone. This is a super-simple and very delicious morning treat. Enjoy it with yogurt or milk, or just eat it on its own. This is also a great recipe to get your little one involved. Have him dump in the ingredients and help you stir it up.

variation

If nut allergies aren't a problem for your family, try the peanut butter version. To make **Peanut Butter Granola,** replace the oil with natural peanut butter. Add peanut butter and maple syrup separately.

6 cups rolled or old-fashioned oats

$^1/_2$ cup uncooked quinoa, rinsed and dried

$^3/_4$ cup raw pumpkin seeds

$^3/_4$ cup raw sunflower seeds

2 tsp. ground cinnamon

$^1/_4$ tsp. salt

$^1/_2$ cup unsweetened coconut flakes (optional)

$^1/_2$ cup grapeseed or canola oil

$^1/_2$ cup maple syrup

1 cup raisins or dried fruit

1. Line a baking sheet with parchment paper. Preheat oven to 325°F (170°C).

2. In a very large bowl, combine oats, quinoa, pumpkin seeds, sunflower seeds, cinnamon, salt, and coconut flakes, if using.

3. In a liquid measuring cup, pour in oil followed by maple syrup. Add to the oat mixture. Stir until oat mixture is coated with liquid.

4. Spread oat mixture in an even layer in the prepared pan. Bake for 40 to 50 minutes, until golden brown. Stir every 15 minutes to make sure it does not burn. Let cool on a cooling rack until room temperature.

5. Add raisins or dried fruit to cooled oat mixture and transfer to a large, airtight container. Store in the fridge for up to 2 months.

pumpkin pie steel-cut oats

This warmly spiced morning treat tastes like pumpkin pie with a little more texture (and a lot more nutrition). It's a largely hands-off recipe, with the slow cooker doing most of the work. By employing the double-boiler method, you don't have to worry about the oats burning, and it makes for an easy cleanup.

PREP	10 minutes
COOK	7 hours
YIELD	6 cups
SERVING SIZE	1/3 cup
SPECIAL TOOLS	slow cooker

1 cup steel-cut oats

1 cup pumpkin purée

2 cups milk or non-dairy milk

1 1/2 cups water

1/2 cup unsweetened applesauce

1/2 cup maple syrup

1 TB. pumpkin pie spice

1 tsp. ground cinnamon

1 tsp. vanilla extract

1/4 tsp. salt

1. Grease an oven-proof 1 1/2-quart bowl or casserole dish with butter or cooking spray. The bowl or dish you use must be able to fit inside your slow cooker with the lid on.

2. In a large bowl, combine all ingredients. Pour into prepared bowl.

3. Fill a large slow cooker about halfway with water. Place bowl with oat mixture in the slow cooker, making sure water does not get into the mixture. Cook on low for 7 hours.

4. Store leftovers in the fridge for up to 1 week.

18 to 24 months

pumpkin chocolate *protein bars*

These have been a family favorite since before Baby G. My husband and I would make a variation of these whenever we traveled. They are a great on-the-go snack. The protein is filling and the chocolate chips make it feel like a treat. For this version, I made a few tweaks to make it more palatable to little ones.

PREP	20 minutes
COOK	20 to 25 minutes
YIELD	16 bars
SERVING SIZE	½ bar

2 cups whole-wheat pastry flour

¼ cup rolled oats

1 TB. pumpkin pie spice

2 tsp. ground cinnamon

1 tsp. ground nutmeg

2 tsp. baking powder

¼ tsp. salt

1 (15 oz.; 425g) can pumpkin purée

¾ cup firm tofu

3 TB. maple syrup

1 TB. vanilla extract

½ cup mini chocolate chips

1. Preheat oven to 350°F (180°C). Grease a 9×9-inch (23×23cm) pan.

2. In a large bowl, whisk together whole-wheat pastry flour, oats, pumpkin pie spice, cinnamon, nutmeg, baking powder, and salt.

3. In a blender, combine pumpkin purée, tofu, maple syrup, and vanilla extract and blend until smooth.

4. Add pumpkin mixture to dry ingredients and stir until combined. Fold in mini chocolate chips. Batter will be very thick. Pour into the prepared pan.

5. Bake for 20 to 25 minutes or until the top is cracked and a toothpick inserted into the center of the pan comes out clean.

6. Store in the fridge for up to 2 weeks or in the freezer for up to 3 months.

note

If you taste the batter, it will be bitter. Once baked, the chocolate chips will add their sweetness. Also note that the texture of these bars is very moist, much more than a typical pumpkin bar. The bars are done when a toothpick inserted in the middle comes out clean. Don't overbake them.

18 to 24 months

pumpkin oat *bars*

PREP	15 minutes
COOK	25 to 30 minutes
YIELD	28 bars
SERVING SIZE	1 bar

These are my go-to pumpkin snack. With just enough sweetness to make it a treat and plenty of whole grains, this bar is a win-win for the whole family. I love adding chopped pecans for texture, but you can omit them for toothless little ones or for those with nut allergies.

½ cup unsalted butter, room temperature

1 cup dark brown sugar, packed

1 (14.5-oz.; 411g) can pumpkin puree

3 large eggs

2 cups whole-wheat pastry flour

1 cup rolled oats

2½ tsp. baking soda

½ TB. pumpkin pie spice

½ tsp. ground cinnamon

¼ tsp. salt

1 cup finely chopped pecans (optional)

1. Preheat the oven to 350°F (180°C). Grease a 10×15-inch (25×38cm) cake pan.

2. In the bowl of a stand mixer, cream butter and sugar for about 1 minute or until light and fluffy. This may take longer if you use a handheld mixer or mix by hand.

3. Add pumpkin purée and eggs and beat on low speed until well combined.

4. In a medium bowl, whisk together whole-wheat pastry flour, oats, baking soda, pumpkin pie spice, cinnamon, and salt. Add half of the pumpkin mixture and stir just until combined. Repeat with remaining pumpkin mixture. Fold in pecans, if using.

5. Pour mixture into the prepared cake pan, and bake for 25 to 30 minutes or until a toothpick inserted into the center comes out with 1 or 2 crumbs on it. Bars will continue baking as they cool, so try not to wait until the toothpick comes out clean.

6. Cool bars completely in the cake pan.

7. Store in airtight container in the fridge for up to 1 week or at room temperature for 3 to 4 days.

salsa eggs

They say that babies gravitate toward the mother ate during pregnancy. When I was pregnant, I ate eggs at almost every meal and craved spicy food, so this recipe is a natural for Baby G and me. My husband and I love eating it over a bed of shredded lettuce. All of us enjoy eating it with tortilla chips and a little shredded cheese.

PREP	2 minutes
COOK	15 to 20 minutes
YIELD	5 cups
SERVING SIZE	1 egg + $\frac{1}{4}$ cup salsa

3 cups salsa   4 eggs

1. Pour salsa in a medium sauté pan with high sides. Make four indentations in the salsa, and crack an egg into each indentation.

2. Cover the pan and cook over medium-low heat for 15 to 20 minutes, until eggs are set. After eggs begin to cook, use a spatula to break the yolk on each egg. This will make it easier to see when the eggs are done.

3. Serve immediately with shredded cheese, tortilla chips, and shredded lettuce. This is not a great leftover meal, so eat up!

note
If you prefer egg whites, separate the eggs and add just the whites to the pan.

selecting salsa
Chunky salsas work best for this recipe. Other than that, choose your favorite salsa, but keep an eye on the ingredients. All the ingredients should be whole foods, and steer clear of added sugar. Select a spice level with your little one in mind. Some kiddos can tolerate a medium salsa, but err on the mild side.

ham salad

PREP	10 minutes
YIELD	2 cups
SERVING SIZE	2 table-spoons
SPECIAL TOOLS	food processor

This is a great way to use up leftover ham and makes a savory spread for tea sandwiches or crackers. The food processor makes the prep easy and the texture just right for little mouths. You don't have to wait for a holiday to make this ham salad. A common weeknight meal for our family is a ham steak with fried eggs and hash browns. Then we have plenty of ham for tasty ham salad!

1 cup cooked ham, roughly chopped

1/4 medium onion, peeled

1 rib celery, roughly chopped

1/8 red pepper

1/4 cup mayonnaise

2 TB. pickle relish (sweet or dill) or diced pickles

1 tsp. yellow mustard

1/4 tsp. salt

1/4 tsp. ground black pepper

1 tsp. apple cider vinegar

1. In a food processor fitted with a chopping blade, pulse the ham until it is in bite-size pieces. Add onion, celery, and red pepper. Pulse until finely chopped.

2. Transfer ham and veggie mixture to a medium bowl. Add mayonnaise, pickle relish, yellow mustard, salt, pepper, and apple cider vinegar. Stir to combine.

3. Serve immediately. Store leftovers in an airtight container in the fridge for up to 5 days.

chicken *salad*

PREP	15 minutes
YIELD	2 cups
SERVING SIZE	1/4 cup

When I have leftover chicken, this is one of my go-to recipes. The dill pickle relish adds a flavorful zing, but you can substitute sweet pickle relish if you prefer. Just be sure to buy a brand that doesn't include high-fructose corn syrup.

1 cup cooked chicken, finely chopped

1 TB. medium sweet onion, grated

1/2 medium carrot, grated

2 TB. dill pickle relish or finely diced dill pickles

1/4 medium avocado, mashed

1 1/2 TB. mayonnaise

1 tsp. yellow mustard

1. In a small bowl, combine all ingredients and gently mix together. Serve immediately.

2. Store leftovers in a covered container in the fridge for up to 2 days.

variations

To make **Egg-Free Chicken Salad,** substitute Greek yogurt for the mayonnaise.

To make **Tuna Salad,** substitute tuna for chicken and add 2 tablespoons of finely diced celery.

18 to 24 months

honey mustard green beans

I have a confession: green beans are not my favorite vegetable. My daughter is happy to munch on lightly steamed green beans tossed with lemon and olive oil, but I need a little more convincing. This sweet and tangy honey mustard dressing makes me excited about boring old green beans. The sesame seeds add a nice crunch, and suddenly vegetables seem a lot more like a treat.

PREP	10 minutes
COOK	5 minutes
YIELD	2 cups
SERVING SIZE	3 to 6 beans

3 TB. mild oil (grapeseed or canola)

2 TB. mayonnaise

2 TB. yellow mustard

2 TB. honey

2 cups green beans, washed and ends removed

½ to 1 cup water

1½ tsp. sesame seeds

1. In a small jar with a tight-fitting lid, combine oil, mayonnaise, yellow mustard, and honey. Shake to combine.

2. Place green beans in the basket of a microwave steamer and add ½ to 1 cup water to the base. Microwave on high for 3 to 4 minutes.

3. In a medium bowl, toss steamed green beans with 1 to 3 tablespoons dressing and sesame seeds. Serve immediately, or cool and serve at room temperature. Store leftover dressing in the fridge for up to 2 weeks.

tip
You can use the honey mustard dressing for more than just green beans. It's perfect for dipping chicken nuggets or veggies, or for topping a green salad. Store in the fridge for up to 2 weeks.

18 to 24 months

potato *salad*

Creamy potatoes, bright red pepper, and crunchy celery come together in this classic Midwestern potato salad adorned simply with mayonnaise and yellow mustard. If you have a hard-boiled egg in the fridge, add it to the salad, but it will be just fine without it. Both this recipe and the sweet potato variation take a little time for prep, but it's mostly hands off.

PREP	30 to 40 minutes
COOK	5 minutes
YIELD	1 quart (1l)
SERVING SIZE	1/3 cup

3 red potatoes, peeled and cut into bite-size pieces (about 3 cups)

1 rib celery, quartered

1/8 white onion

1/4 sweet red pepper, seeds and stem removed

1 hard-boiled egg, chopped (optional)

1/4 cup mayonnaise

1 tsp. yellow mustard

1 TB. fresh lemon juice

1/4 tsp. ground black pepper

1/4 tsp. salt

1. Place potatoes in a saucepan and cover with 1 inch (2.5cm) cold water. Bring to a boil over high heat and then reduce heat to medium-low and cover. Simmer for 10 minutes. Drain and rinse with cold water. Cool to room temperature.

2. While the potatoes are cooking, add the onion, celery, and red pepper to a food processor fitted with a chopping blade. Pulse until veggies are finely diced. Remove any large pieces and discard.

3. When the potatoes are cool, toss them with vegetable mixture, mayonnaise, yellow mustard, egg (if using), and lemon juice. Season with ground black pepper and salt. Serve immediately. Store leftovers in the fridge for up to 3 days.

variations

For **Smoky Sweet Potato Salad,** replace the red potatoes with 1 large sweet potato, peeled and cut into 1/2-inch (1.25cm) cubes (approximately 3 cups). Line a baking sheet with foil. Toss sweet potato cubes with 1/2 TB. grapeseed or canola oil, 1/4 tsp. salt, 1/4 tsp. ground black pepper, and 1/4 tsp. smoked paprika. Roast at 400°F (200°C) for 30 minutes. Let cool to room temperature and proceed with recipe, substituting 1 TB. apple cider vinegar for lemon juice.

To make these recipes **Egg-Free,** substitute Greek yogurt for the mayonnaise and omit hard-boiled egg.

salad *dressings*

Homemade dressings make salad greens more appealing to little ones, and you avoid the sugar and other unnecessary ingredients found in store-bought brands. This Carrot Ginger Dressing gets its sweetness from the carrots and a little zing from the ginger. Creamy Poppy Seed Vinaigrette is sweet and savory and pairs perfectly with spinach and baby kale as well as fruits like diced apple, pomegranate seeds, strawberries, or sliced grapes.

18 to 24 months

carrot ginger *dressing*

PREP	25 to 30 minutes
YIELD	2 cups
SERVING SIZE	1 tablespoon

- 2 medium carrots, grated, or 2 cups shredded carrots
- 2 TB. fresh ginger, peeled and chopped
- 2 TB. sesame oil
- 1/3 cup grapeseed oil or olive oil
- 1/4 cup apple cider vinegar
- 1 TB. soy sauce
- 1 to 2 tsp. honey
- 1 small clove garlic, minced
- 1/4 cup water

1. Combine carrots, ginger, sesame oil, grapeseed or olive oil, vinegar, soy sauce, honey, and garlic in a blender. Blend until smooth.

2. Add water and blend to desired consistency. If you want a thicker dressing, omit the water.

3. Store leftovers in the fridge for up to 2 weeks.

creamy poppy seed *vinaigrette*

PREP	10 minutes
YIELD	2 cups
SERVING SIZE	1 tablespoon

- 3/4 cup oil (olive, canola, or grapeseed)
- 1/2 cup apple cider vinegar
- 3 TB. mayonnaise
- 1/4 cup granulated sugar
- 1 1/2 tsp. ground mustard
- 1/4 tsp. onion powder
- 1 tsp. salt
- 2 TB. poppy seeds

1. Combine all ingredients in a blender. Blend until mixture is creamy and smooth.

2. Store in an airtight container in the fridge for up to 2 weeks.

baked falafel

The key to making your own falafel lies in the chickpeas. Unfortunately, canned beans cause soggy falafel. The trick is soaking the chickpeas for 12 to 16 hours. It's as easy as throwing them in water before bed and baking the falafel at lunch. This is a great finger food, especially with ketchup and yogurt dipping sauce. For bigger kids, fold the falafel in a whole-wheat tortilla and top with shredded lettuce and tomatoes.

PREP	15 minutes plus 12 to 16 hours soaking
COOK	20 to 30 minutes
YIELD	12 to 15 patties
SERVING SIZE	2 patties
SPECIAL TOOLS	food processor

1 cup dried chickpeas

2 TB. olive oil

¼ medium red onion

½ cup fresh cilantro, roughly chopped

Juice of 1 lemon, about ¼ cup

1 clove garlic

1 tsp. ground cumin

1. Place chickpeas in a medium bowl. Cover with several inches of water. Let soak for 12 to 16 hours.

2. Pour 2 TB. oil on a rimmed baking sheet. Place in oven. Preheat oven to 375°F (190°C).

3. In a food processor fitted with a chopping blade, combine soaked chickpeas, onion, cilantro, lemon juice, garlic, and cumin. Pulse until mixture is a chunky purée. You should still see pieces of the chickpeas.

4. Once oven is preheated, remove cookie sheet. Form falafel into 2-inch (5cm) patties by scooping out with a spoon and flattening with your hand. Place on cookie sheet.

5. Bake 12 to 15 minutes. Flip carefully and bake an additional 10 to 12 minutes until golden brown. Let cool to room temperature and serve.

6. Store leftovers in the fridge for up to 3 days or in the freezer for up to 3 months. To reheat from frozen, wrap in foil and reheat at 350°F (180°C) for 15 to 30 minutes until heated through.

cucumber yogurt sauce

Combine ½ cup plain or Greek yogurt, ¼ cup diced cucumber, and juice of ½ lemon. Mix well.

18 to 24 months

roasted broccoli and cauliflower

PREP	20 minutes
COOK	25 minutes
YIELD	4 to 5 cups
SERVING SIZE	1/4 cup

If your little one will only eat broccoli when it's drenched in cheese sauce, give this recipe a try. Here, the cheese does not camouflage the flavor of the veggies, but enhances the nuttiness that comes from the roasting. This is a recipe for the whole family—big kids and adults will love the complex and comforting flavors; little kids will love the cheese and the soft texture of the vegetables.

1 head broccoli, cut into bite-size pieces

1 head cauliflower, cut into bite-size pieces

6 TB. grapeseed oil

6 TB. Seasoned Breadcrumbs (see sidebar)

1/4 cup Parmesan cheese

1/4 cup cheddar cheese, shredded

1. Preheat oven to 425°F (220°C). Line a rimmed baking sheet with parchment paper.

2. In a zipper-lock bag, add broccoli, 3 TB. oil, and 3 TB. seasoned breadcrumbs. Seal and shake until ingredients are well combined.

3. In a separate zipper-lock bag, combine cauliflower, remaining 3 TB. oil, and remaining 3 TB. breadcrumbs. Seal and shake until ingredients are well combined.

4. Spread cauliflower on prepared sheet. Bake for 15 minutes. Add broccoli. Bake for an additional 10 minutes. Turn the oven off. Remove the broccoli and cauliflower.

5. Add Parmesan and cheddar cheeses and toss to combine. Return to warm oven for 1 minute. Serve immediately.

6. Leftovers can be refrigerated in an airtight container for up to 2 days.

nutritional note

It's wise to get your kids started on broccoli and cauliflower at a young age. Both are rich in several important nutrients including vitamin C, vitamin K, and fiber. They also contain powerful anti-cancer nutrients. Broccoli is one of the few vegetables that provides moderate amounts of calcium.

18 to 24 months

seasoned breadcrumbs

2 cups panko breadcrumbs

2 tsp. salt

1 tsp. sugar

$\frac{1}{4}$ tsp. white ground pepper

$\frac{1}{2}$ tsp. ground mustard

$\frac{1}{2}$ tsp. chili powder

$\frac{1}{2}$ tsp. garlic powder

1 tsp. onion powder

1 tsp. Italian seasoning

3 TB. mild oil (grapeseed oil, canola oil)

In a small bowl, whisk all ingredients. Store in an airtight container at room temperature for up to 1 month, or in the freezer for up to 6 months. Use leftover breadcrumbs for Chicken Nuggets or Fish Sticks.

chicken *nuggets*

PREP	10 minutes
COOK	15 to 20 minutes
YIELD	15 to 18 nuggets
SERVING SIZE	1 to 2 nuggets

These crispy nuggets are easy to throw together, and taste way better than anything you can find in the freezer section. Say goodbye to egg washes and messy preparation. All your prep is done in a freezer bag with just water adhering the seasoning to the chicken.

2 cups panko bread-crumbs

2 tsp. salt

1 tsp. sugar

¼ tsp. ground white pepper

½ tsp. ground mustard

½ tsp. chili powder

½ tsp. garlic powder

1 tsp. onion powder

1 tsp. Italian seasoning or ½ tsp. dried basil and ½ tsp. ground oregano

3 TB. mild oil (grape-seed oil, canola oil)

1 lb. (450g) chicken breast tenders

1. Preheat oven to 400°F (200°C). Line a rimmed baking sheet with parchment paper and spray the parchment paper with oil spray.

2. In a large bowl, use a fork to whisk together breadcrumbs, salt, sugar, ground white pepper, ground mustard, chili powder, garlic powder, onion powder, and Italian seasoning. Add oil and whisk until mixture is no longer clumpy.

3. Cut chicken tenders into bite-size pieces. Rinse with water. Shake off excess water and place in a zipper-lock bag.

4. Add half of breadcrumb mixture to chicken tenders. Seal the bag and shake until mixture is dispersed and adhered to the chicken. Add more breadcrumb mixture as needed and repeat until tenders are coated evenly in breadcrumb mixture.

5. Place chicken tenders on prepared baking sheet. Bake for 15 to 20 minutes until breading is crisp and golden, and the chicken has reached an internal temperature for 165°F (75°C). Serve with ketchup, barbecue sauce, or homemade ranch dip.

6. Store leftovers in an airtight container for up to 5 days in the fridge or up to 1 month in the freezer. To reheat from frozen, bake for 10 to 15 minutes at 400°F (200°C).

make it ahead

The breadcrumb mixture can be stored in the pantry for up to 1 week, or in the freezer for up to 6 months. You can also prep the chicken up to a day in advance and store in a zipper-lock bag in the fridge until din-nertime. Just add the breadcrumbs right before you are ready to bake them.

18 to 24 months

dill *dip*

I have found the best way to get my daughter to eat vegetables is to eat vegetables in front of her. As much as I would love to say that I happily munch on plain, raw carrots and celery, it just doesn't happen. I need some dip. This is one of my favorite dips and it also goes well with plain potato chips.

½ cup mayonnaise	1 TB. dried dill	½ tsp. sugar
¾ cup sour cream or Greek yogurt	½ tsp. onion powder	
	½ tsp. seasoned salt	

1. In a medium bowl, mix all ingredients until combined. Refrigerate for at least 30 minutes so flavors can meld.

2. Serve with raw vegetables. Store in the fridge for up to 1 week.

PREP	5 minutes plus 30 minutes to chill
YIELD	1¼ cups
SERVING SIZE	2 table-spoons

ranch *dip*

Ranch dip is a great way to encourage kiddos to eat veggies or chicken nuggets. The seasoning mix used for this dip can be made in advance and kept in the pantry for up to 3 months. All you need to do is mix it with sour cream or yogurt.

¼ cup dried parsley	1 tsp. dried minced onion	1 tsp. seasoned salt
2 tsp. onion powder	1 tsp. garlic powder	½ cup sour cream or Greek yogurt

1. In a small bowl, mix parsley, onion powder, dried minced onion, garlic powder, and seasoned salt with a fork until combined. Use immediately or store in an airtight container away from sunlight for up to 3 months.

2. When you are ready to make dip, mix ½ TB. seasoning with ½ cup sour cream or yogurt. Store in the fridge for up to 5 days.

PREP	10 minutes
YIELD	½ cup
SERVING SIZE	2 table-spoons

substitution
If dairy is a problem, substitute mayonnaise for the sour cream.

tartar sauce

To make tartar sauce for dipping, combine ½ cup mayonnaise, 3 TB. dill pickle relish or chopped dill pickles, ½ tsp. sugar, juice of 1 lemon, and a dash of hot sauce.

fish *sticks*

Solid pieces of cod and a crunchy, savory coating make these homemade fish sticks much tastier and healthier than their freezer-section counterparts.

1½ lb. (680g) cod, cut into strips

1 cup whole-wheat pastry flour

2 cups panko bread-crumbs

2 tsp. salt

1 tsp. sugar

¼ tsp. ground white pepper

½ tsp. ground mustard

½ tsp. chili powder

½ tsp. garlic powder

1 tsp onion powder

1 tsp. Italian seasoning

5 TB. mild oil (grape-seed or canola oil)

4 egg whites

PREP	40 minutes
COOK	15 to 20 minutes
YIELD	20 to 24 fish sticks
SERVING SIZE	1 to 2 fish sticks

1. Place flour in a shallow bowl and set up a cooling rack. Dredge fish sticks in flour and then place on rack to dry for 20 minutes. Discard any unused flour.

2. In a large bowl, use a fork to mix together breadcrumbs, salt, sugar, ground white pepper, ground mustard, chili powder, garlic powder, onion powder, and Italian seasoning. Add 3 TB. oil and whisk until mixture is no longer clumpy. Transfer half of the breadcrumb mixture to a shallow bowl.

3. In another shallow bowl, whisk 4 egg whites until well combined. Get out another cooling rack.

4. Dredge the flour-coated fish sticks in the egg whites and then in breadcrumbs, using your hand to press breadcrumbs into the fish. Place the dredged fish sticks onto the new cooling rack.

5. Let the fish sticks dry for at least 20 minutes and up to 8 hours. If drying longer than 20 minutes, place the rack with the fish sticks on a rimmed baking sheet and refrigerate.

6. Pour the remaining 2 TB. oil on a rimmed baking sheet. Place sheet in oven and preheat oven to 400°F (200°C). Remove pan and place fish sticks on pan. Bake for 10 to 15 minutes until breadcrumbs are starting to turn golden and fish is cooked through. Serve immediately.

7. Store leftovers in the fridge for up to 1 day or in the freezer for up to 1 month. Reheat in oven at 350°F (180°C). From fridge, reheat for 15 minutes; from frozen, 25 minutes.

tip

This recipe calls for the fish sticks to "dry" between stages. If you are in a hurry, skip these steps. The bread-ing may not adhere quite as well, but they will still be good.

18 to 24 months

beef and tomato *pasta bake*

PREP	30 minutes
COOK	45 minutes
YIELD	3 quarts (3l)
SERVING SIZE	½ cup

note

To make a dairy-free version, do not add the cheese and make sure that your tomato soup does not include dairy.

This was my favorite meal growing up: tangy tomatoes, savory ground beef, sweet kernels of corn, salty mushrooms, and soft elbow noodles—in other words, Midwestern comfort in a dish. It can be made up to a day in advance and it freezes well, so it's perfect for a busy night or when your kiddo will be with a babysitter.

3 medium carrots, diced

4 celery stalks, diced

2 medium onions, diced

1 lb. (450g) 100% grass-fed ground beef

½ tsp. salt

½ tsp. ground black pepper

8 oz. (225g) whole-wheat elbow macaroni

32 oz. (950g) tomato soup

1 (14.5-oz.; 411g) can diced tomatoes

1 cup frozen corn

1 (8 oz.; 225g) can mushrooms

1½ cup shredded cheddar cheese

1. Preheat oven to 350°F (180°C).

2. Cook the macaroni according to package directions. Drain but do not rinse.

3. While the macaroni is cooking, sauté the onion, carrots, and celery in a large frying pan over medium-high heat until softened, about 10 minutes. Add ground beef and cook until brown. Season with salt and ground black pepper.

4. In a 9×11-inch (23×28cm) or 3-quart (3l) dish, combine macaroni, beef mixture, tomato soup, diced tomatoes, mushrooms, and corn. Top with shredded cheese.

5. Bake for 35 to 45 minutes until cheese is melted and dish is heated through. Serve immediately. Store in the fridge for up to 5 days or freeze for up to 3 months.

make it ahead

I always prep this dish during naptime and add the cheese right before throwing it in the oven. You could even make it the night before. If you plan to freeze some of the dish, do not add cheese to that portion. To reheat from frozen, thaw in the fridge overnight and reheat in a saucepan over medium heat or in the microwave.

tofu taco *filling*

This is one of our go-to, flexible weeknight meals. Super hungry? Just heat it enough to warm it up. Trying to get a few things done before dinner? Simmer for closer to 30 minutes and let the salsa cook down to a concentrated sauce.

PREP	10 minutes
COOK	15 to 30 minutes
YIELD	4 to 5 cups
SERVING SIZE	1/3 cup

2 (15-oz.; 420g) jars salsa

14 oz. (400g) firm tofu, cut in 1-inch (2.5cm) cubes

8 oz. (225g) sliced mushrooms (optional)

1. In a medium frying pan with a high rim, combine salsa, tofu, and mushrooms (if using). Stir ingredients so that the tofu is covered in salsa.

2. Cook over medium heat for 15 to 30 minutes, stirring occasionally. Serve immediately. Store leftovers in the fridge for up to 3 days.

serving suggestion
Serve over salad, in a corn tortilla, or as a hearty dip with tortilla chips. Top with shredded cheddar cheese, Greek yogurt or sour cream, sliced avocado, and shredded lettuce.

18 to 24 months

blueberry doughnuts

PREP	15 minutes
COOK	12 to 15 minutes
YIELD	8 dough-nuts
SERVING SIZE	½ doughnut
SPECIAL TOOLS	doughnut pan

Just because you are trying to make healthy food for your kiddo does not mean treats are off limits. I am a firm believer in healthier treats. Would an apple be better for your kiddo? No question in my mind. However, some-times only a doughnut will suffice. And when that dough-nut is made with nutrient-rich blueberries, who minds a little white chocolate frosting?

2 cups whole-wheat pastry flour

1 TB. baking powder

1½ tsp. ground nutmeg

½ tsp. ground cinnamon

¼ tsp. salt

½ cup sugar

½ cup milk or non-dairy milk

1 cup frozen blueberries, thawed

2 TB. butter, melted

1 cup white chocolate or milk chocolate chips

1 TB. canola or grape-seed oil

note

These doughnuts are based on a recipe from one of my favorite vegan bakers, Mama Pea (Sarah Matheny). If you are looking for some great egg-free treats, check out her books, *Peas and Thank You* and *More Peas, Thank You.*

1. Preheat oven to 350°F (180°C). Grease a doughnut pan.

2. In a large bowl, whisk together whole-wheat pastry flour, baking powder, nutmeg, cinnamon, and salt.

3. In a blender, purée sugar, milk, and blueberries until smooth. Pour blue-berry mixture into flour mixture and stir to combine. Add melted butter and stir to combine.

4. Pour into prepared pan. Bake for 12 to 15 minutes until you can insert a toothpick in a doughnut and it comes out clean. Set pan on cooling rack and allow to cool for 5 to 10 minutes. Then run a butter knife around the edges to loosen the doughnuts and invert onto the cooling rack.

5. As doughnuts cool, place a piece of wax paper under the cooling rack. Place chocolate chips and oil in a medium microwave-safe bowl. Microwave on high for 30 seconds, stir, and microwave for 15 seconds. Continue stirring and microwaving for 15-second intervals until choco-late is melted and smooth.

6. Dip the top of each doughnut into the melted white chocolate. Let cool until chocolate hardens. Store in the fridge for up to 1 week or in the freezer for up to 1 month.

index

numbers

a

q–r

t

u–v

w–x–y–z

photo credits

Pages 28-29: Ian O'Leary © Dorling Kindersley and
    William Reavell © Dorling Kindersley

All other photos by Stephanie Kelley Photography
    © Dorling Kindersley